Air Fryer Cookbook

Quick, Healthy and Delicious Recipes. Discover the Ultimate Technology to Cook Your Favorite Fried Food.

Elizabeth Baker

Table Of Contents

CHAPTER-3: AIR FRYER APPETIZER RECIPES 45

CHAPTER-4: DESSERT RECIPES 71

Introduction

An air-fryer is a modern kitchen appliance that cooks food by blowing extremely hot air around this machine instead of using oil. Conveniently this allows a low-fat version of food that would usually be fried in a deep fryer. As a result, fatty foods like fries, fried chicken, and curly fries are typically cooked with no oil or up to 80percent less fat than mainstream conventional cooking methods.

The Air Fryer provides fried foods and healthy meals, allowing you to avoid the calories associated with fried foods while still getting the glamour of food through crunch, taste, and flavors you want. Unlike others, the household appliance works by blowing very hot air (up to 400 ° F) evenly and quickly around with a food ingredient placed in an enclosed space. The heat allows the outside of the food to be crispy and brittle; however, the inside remains soft and moist. An air fryer can be used for almost anything. Furthermore, in addition to frying, you are also open to the option of a barbecue, baking, and roast- Its variety of cooking options makes it easier to consume more meals suited for any time of day.

What you get out of this change?

At this stage, you may feel a little hesitant to make this change, and that is completely understandable, however after being exposed to how air-frying not only has its health benefits and how it is flexible to the extent that it shapes your life providing fast, but innovative food also that we often miss out on in the wreck and rummage of 21st-century life, you're bound to be blown away and reflect on your own current nutritional choices. Our motive is to help take a step towards a change in healthy lifestyles- wait till you see our delicious food section!

Chapter -1: What Is Air Fryer?

The air fryer is a cooktop convective oven with more power. (However, there is a distinction between air-frying and baking.) The small gadget claims to replicate deep-frying effects using only hot air and little or no oil.

And according to market researchers, approximately 40% of homes in the United States had one as of July 2020. Anything from frozen chicken nuggets and French fries to roasted vegetables and fresh-baked cookies can be air-fried.

1.1 What makes an air fryer different from a deep fryer?

Deep fryers cook the food in a vat of oil that has been heated to a specific temperature, while air fryers bake food at an extreme temperature with such a high-powered fan. Both cook food fast, but an air fryer takes almost no time to preheat, while a deep fryer will take up to 10 minutes. Air fryers use little or no oil, while deep fryers use a lot of oil that absorbs into the food. Food in both machines comes out juicy, crispy, and tasty, but they taste different since deep-fried foods are coated in batter, which looks different in an air fryer than it does in a deep fryer. In an air fryer, sprayed foods need to be sprayed with oil before frying to make them flavor and crisp up, while in a deep fryer, the hot oil soaks into the batter. In an air fryer, wet batters and flour-based batters don't perform as well as they do in a deep fryer.

1.2 Is air-fried food good for you?

Air-fried food has a similar flavor and texture to deep-fried food: crisp on the outside, juicy and tasty from the inside. However, based on what you're cooking, you'll only need a small amount of oil, if at all.

Yeah, air frying is "definitely a better choice to deep frying if you agree to use only 1-2 tablespoons of a plant-based oil with spices, and you stick to air-frying vegetables rather than anything else," says Jaclyn London, MS, RD, CDN, of Good

Housekeeping. "Any appliance that encourages you and your family to eat more vegetables is essential for weight loss, lowering the risk of developing chronic diseases, and improving long-term health as we get older.

1.3 Is it worth investing in an air fryer?

First and foremost, decide if you need a new appliance. Many toaster ovens, such as the smart oven air, and some pressure cookers, such as the Ninja Foodie, even have air frying capabilities.

If you ever plan to invest in an air fryer, keep in mind that they will cost anything from $40 for a small compact model to $400 for a large air fryer toaster oven. Remember how often people you'll be cooking for a while looking for an air fryer: The smallest air fryers (1.2 liters) can serve 1-2 persons, while the medium sizes (3--0.4) can serve 2-3 people and the biggest (6 liters or more) can serve 4-6 people. Since air fryers with baskets cook more uniformly than those with shelves, we prefer them.

1.4 How do air fryers work?

An air fryer isn't the same as a traditional fryer. It cooks food differently than deep frying. It cooks food a little faster, uniformly distributes heat, and suspends it in a thin metal basket. It can help speed it up — perhaps you just need some healthy food quickly, McManus says.

Many models do not need preheating, which saves time and allows food to be cooked easily. They won't heat your kitchen as much as your oven would in hotter climates or during the summer months.

A heating process and a fan are housed in the top portion of an air fryer. When you turn on the fryer, hot air rushes down and around the food in a fryer-style basket. The food becomes crisp due to the fast circulation, which is similar to deep-frying except without the oil.

The following are some tips for using an air fryer:

1. Place the basket with your food:

The basket will carry anything from 2 to 10 quarts, depending on the size of your air fryer. In most cases, 1 or 2 teaspoons of oil will be required to help the food become crispy.

2. Settle time and temperature:

Depending on the food you're frying, air fryer cooking methods and temperatures vary from 5 to 25 mins at 350° to 400°F.

3. Allow the food to cook:

To help the food crisp up evenly, you will need to flip or transform it halfway through cooking. It's necessary to clean your air fryer after you've finished cooking.

TRY IT!

9 FOODS YOU SHOULD AIR-FRY

Because of the unique way an air fryer cooks, it's one of the most versatile appliances we've tested. Trust it to perfectly melt cheese, cook delicate meats and more.

Grilled Cheese

S'mores

Burgers

Nachos

Lobster Tails

Pork Chops

Salmon

Veggie Tots

Cauliflower Gnocchi

1.5 Why Do You Use It?

Low-Fat Food: The air fryer's most valuable function is that it uses hot-air ventilation to cook food in all directions, eliminating the need for fuel and makes it much easier on a low-fat diet to enjoy delicious, well-balanced recipes without risking their health.

Exceptionally safe: Do you realize how extra careful you must be when tossing chicken or other ingredients into the deep fryer? Since it's still really hot outside, you want to make sure the hot oil doesn't spill and burn your skin. You won't have to worry about brunette skin with your air fryer due to hot oil spillage.

The air fryer allows you to multitask because it can cook several dishes at once. It's your one-stop-shop for all your grilling, baking, frying, and roasting needs! You don't need many gadgets for different tasks any longer.

Healthier Foods: Air fryers are designed to cook without fattening oils, resulting in healthier foods with up to 80% less fat. It allows you to lose weight by eating fried foods while maintaining calories and saturated fat. Making a move to a healthier lifestyle is easier with the help of this device. The odor of deep-fried foods, which lingers in the room for hours after they've been deep-fried, is also removed from your home.

Tips for Usage:

- Preheat your fryer before use
- Always cook in batches. Do not overcrowd your fryer
- Space Your Foods evenly when added to the air fryer
- Keep It Dry

Use spray oil to oil your food.

Chapter-2: Breakfast Recipes

1.Apple Fritters

Time to prepare: 6-7 minutes

Cooking time: 5 minutes

Servings: 6

Ingredients

- Spray can of cooking oil

- 1 1/2 cups flour (all-purpose)

- 1 tablespoon of sugar

- 2 tablespoons powdered baking soda

- 1 1/2 teaspoons cinnamon powder

- a half teaspoon of salt

- 2/3 cup milk (2% fat)

- 2 big room-temperature eggs

- a quarter-cup of lemon juice

- 1 1/2 teaspoon vanilla extract (distributed)

- 2 medium peeled and chopped Honeycrisp apples

- 1 tablespoon of butter

- 1 cup confectioners' sugar

- 1 tablespoon of milk

Instructions

1. Spray the air-fryer basket and line it with parchment paper (cut to fit)—Preheat the air fryer to 410 degrees Fahrenheit.

2. Combine flour, sugar, baking powder, cinnamon, and salt in a big mixing bowl. Combine the milk, eggs, lemon juice, and 1 teaspoon vanilla extract in a mixing bowl and swirl until combined. Apples should be folded in.

3. Drop dough by 1/4 cupful's 2-in. apart into air-fryer basket in batches. Using cooking spray, spritz the

surface. Cook for 5-6 minutes, or until golden brown. Continue to air-fry fritters until golden brown, around 1-2 minutes.

4. In a small saucepan over medium-high heat, melt the butter. Cook, occasionally stirring, until the butter begins to brown and foam, about 5 minutes. Remove from the heat and allow to cool slightly. Toss the browned butter with the confectioners' sugar, 1 tablespoon milk, and the remaining 1/2 teaspoon vanilla extract; whisk until smooth. Before serving, drizzle the glaze over the cakes.

2.Toast Cups with Air-Fried Ham and Egg

Time to prepare: 6-7 minutes

Cooking time: 15 minutes

Servings: 6

Ingredients

- 4 ramekins

- a dozen eggs

- (8 slices) Toast

- 2 Ham Slicing's

- a stick of butter

- sodium chloride

- cayenne

Instructions

1. Using a cooking brush, coat the inside of the ramekin with a generous amount of butter. The more butter on the toast cups, the easier they are to detach from the ramekins.

2. Using a rolling pin or your palm, flatten 8 slices of toast. It should be as flat as possible.

3. Line insides each ramekin with a slice of flattened toast. There will almost certainly be excess bread folding inwards. However, pinch the extra folds to make the cup as good as possible.

4. Put a second flattened piece of toast on top of the first, pressing down on the extra folds. Cut two ham slices into eight smaller strips.

5. Place 2 ham strips in each ramekin. For a visual representation, see the image above.

6. In each toast cup, crack an egg.

7. Season each egg with salt and black pepper.

8. In the toast cup, you can also put some cheese (as seen above). I used one slice of cheddar cheese, which I cut into small pieces.

9. Bake for 15 minutes at 160 degrees in the Air fryer with all four ramekins. The Air fryer does not need to be preheated.

10. Take ramekins out from the Air fryer using a tea towel, silicone tongs, or whatever kitchen contraception you have to keep your fingers safe from the heat.

To extract the toast cups from the ramekins, carefully sliced around the ramekin inside with a small knife, just if any bread got stuck to the edges, and wriggled the toast cup out of the ramekin with the same tiny knife and spoon.

3. Breakfast Frittata

Time to prepare: 6-7 minutes

Cooking time: 12-16 minutes

Servings: 8

Ingredients

- a dozen eggs

- Cheddar cheese

- Mushrooms

- Tomatoes in grapes (cherry tomatoes)

- spinach, chopped

- herbs, freshly chopped

- Onion green

- sodium chloride

Instructions

1. Preheat the air fryer to 180 degrees Celsius / 350 degrees Fahrenheit.

2. Using parchment paper, line a deep 7-inch baking sheet, then oil it and set it aside.

3. Whisk together the eggs and cream in a mixing dish

4. Toss in the remaining ingredients, including the sea salt flakes, and whisk to mix.

5. Place the baking pan inside the air fryer basket and pour the breakfast frittata mixture into it.

6. Cook it for at least 12-16 minutes or until the eggs are cooked. Place a toothpick into the middle of the air fryer frittata to see if it's finished. If it comes out clean, the eggs are finished.

4.Casserole of Eggs

Time to prepare: 25 minutes

Cooking time: 25 minutes

Servings: 8

Ingredients

- 3 chopped tomatoes for serving

- Season with black pepper and salt

- 2 cup spinach (baby)

- 2 cubed sweet potatoes

- a dozen eggs

- 1 teaspoon cayenne pepper

- 2 tablespoons extra virgin olive oil

- 2-pound ground turkey

Instructions

1. In a large pot, whisk together the eggs, pepper, salt, potato, chili powder, broccoli, sweet potato, and turkey.

2. Preheat your air fryer to 350°F and add the oil.

3. Pour the egg mixture into the air fryer, spread it out evenly, cover, and cook for about 25 minutes.

4. Serve them for brunch by dividing them into individual dishes.

5. Breakfast Casserole with Fruit

Time to prepare: 35 minutes

Cooking time: 5 minutes

Servings: 5

Ingredients

- 1 pound of flour
- 12 teaspoon powdered cinnamon
- 3 tablespoons. granulated sugar
- 5 tablespoons unsalted butter
- 5 tablespoon of Brown sugar

To make the casserole, combine the following ingredients.

- 2 and the third cup of blueberries
- 1 lemon's zest, grated
- 5 tablespoons unsalted butter
- 3 quarts buttermilk
- 1 cup of milk
- 3 eggs
- 2 teaspoon powdered baking soda
- 2 teaspoon bicarbonate of soda
- 3 and 12 cups all-purpose flour
- 3 tablespoons. icing sugar
- 3 eggs

Instructions

1. Whisk together 2 teaspoons white sugar, baking powder, 2 and 12 cups white flour, 2 eggs, baking soda, buttermilk, milk, lemon zest, 4 tablespoons butter, and blueberries in a mixing bowl.

2. In a separate bowl, combine 3 tablespoons brown sugar, 4 tablespoons butter, 2 tablespoons white sugar, cinnamon, 12 cup flour, and whisk until crumbly. Sprinkle over blueberry mixture.

3. Cook for around 30 minutes at about 300 degrees F in a preheated air fryer.

4. Serve them for breakfast by dividing them into bowls. Have fun!

6.Mix sausage, eggs, and cheese

Time to prepare: 5 minutes

Cooking time: 20 minutes

Servings: 6

Ingredients

- Spray for cooking

- Season with black pepper and salt to taste.

- 2 cups of milk

- 10 whisked eggs

- 2 cup shredded mozzarella cheese

- 2 cup shredded cheddar cheese

- 12 ounces fried and crumbled sausages

Instructions:

1. In a mixing bowl, combine the mozzarella, cheese, milk, eggs, pepper, and salt with the sausages.

2. Preheat the air fryer to 380°F, spray the inside with cooking oil, add the sausage mixture and eggs, and cook for about 20 minutes.

3. Cut into thirds and divide among plates. Have fun!

7.Delicious Potato Hash

Time to prepare: 5 minutes

Cooking time:20 minutes

Servings:5

Ingredients

- 2 and 12 cubed potatoes

- 2 chopped yellow onions

- 3 tablespoons of olive oil

- 2 chopped green bell peppers

- Season with black pepper and salt

- 1 teaspoon dried thyme

- 3 eggs

Instructions:

1. Preheat the air fryer to 350°F, add the oil, steam it up, then add the bell pepper, onion, pepper, and salt, mix well, and cook for about five minutes.

2. Stir in the thyme, potatoes, and eggs, then cover and cook for 20 minutes at 360 degrees F.

3. Serve them for brunch by dividing them into bowls. Have fun!

8. Baked Cheese with Air Fryer

Time to prepare: 5 minutes

Cooking time: 20 minutes

Servings: 6

Ingredients

- Spray for cooking

- 5 tablespoons chopped parsley

- Season with black pepper and salt

- 1 teaspoon powdered onion

- 3 eggs

- 2-pound breakfast sausage, taken from casings and chopped

- 3 and 12 cups shredded cheddar cheese

- 3 cups milk

- 6 cooked and crumbled bacon slices

Instructions:

1. In a mixing bowl, thoroughly combine the milk, eggs, onion powder, cheese, pepper, salt, and parsley.

2. Spray your air fryer with cooking spray and heat it to 320 degrees F before adding the bacon and sausage.

3. Scatter the eggs over the top and cook for about 20 minutes.

4. Cut in half and divide between plates. Have fun!

9.Biscuits Casserole

Time to prepare: 5 minutes

Cooking time:15 minutes

Servings: 10

Ingredients

- Spray for cooking

- 3 cups of milk

- Season with black pepper and salt

- 1-pound chopped sausage

- 5 tablespoons of flour

- 14 ounces quartered biscuits

Instructions:

1. Coat the air fryer in cooking oil and preheat it to 350 degrees F.

2. Sprinkle any biscuits on the bottom, then pour in the gravy.

3. Add the milk, flour, pepper, and salt, and cook for about 15 minutes, stirring occasionally.

4. Serve them for brunch by dividing them into bowls. Have fun!

10. Turkey Burrito

Time to prepare: 2-3 minutes

Cooking time: 5 minutes

Servings: 4

Ingredients

- 2/8 cup grind mozzarella cheese

- Season with black pepper and salt

- 6 tablespoons of salsa

- 2 small peeled, pitted, and sliced avocados

- a dozen eggs

- 1 sliced red bell pepper

- 6 pre-cooked turkey breast slices

- Tortillas to be used for serving

Instructions:

1. Beat the eggs in a bowl with some pepper and salt to taste, then transfer to a pan and position in the air fryer basket.

2. Cook for 5 minutes at 400°F, remove the pan from the fryer and transfer the eggs to a plate.

3. Arrange tortillas, broken eggs, turkey meat, cheese, bell pepper, avocado, and salsa on a cutting board.

4. Wrap your burritos in tin foil and place them in the air fryer after you've lined it with tin foil.

5. Warm the burritos in a 350°F oven for about 3 minutes, then break them into plates and eat. Have fun!

11.Tofu Scramble

Preparation time: 10 minutes

Cooking time: 35 minutes

Servings: 6

Ingredients

- Season with black pepper and salt
- 1 cup chopped yellow onion
- 3 and 12 cup cubed red potatoes
- 1 teaspoon powdered garlic
- 1 teaspoon powdered onion 6 cups florets (broccoli)
- 3 tablespoons of olive oil (extra virgin)
- 2 teaspoons of turmeric (ground)
- 2 cubed tofu blocks
- 4 tablespoons Soy sauce

Instructions:

1. Combine the tofu, salt, 1 tablespoon oil, pepper, garlic powder, soy sauce, onion powder, onion, and turmeric in a container, whisk to combine, and set aside.

2. In a small bowl, toss the potatoes with a pinch of salt, the remaining oil, and pepper to cover fully.

3. Preheat your air fryer to 350 degrees F and cook the potatoes for 15 minutes, rotating once.

4. Place the tofu and marinade in your air fryer and cook for 15 minutes.

5. Add the broccoli to the fryer and bake for another 5 minutes.

6. Serve right away. Have fun!

---

12. Oatmeal Casserole

Preparation time: 12 minutes

Cooking time: 25 minutes

Servings: 10

Ingredients

- Spray for cooking

- 2 teaspoon extract de vanilla

- 3 tablespoons unsalted butter

- 2 eggs

- 3 quarts milk

- 2 peeled and mashed bananas

- 1-pound blueberries

- 1 cup cocoa powder

- 2 teaspoon powdered cinnamon

- a 3rd of a cup of brown sugar

- 2 tablespoons powdered baking soda

- 3 cups oats, rolled

Instructions:

1. In a mixing bowl, combine the cinnamon, sugar, baking powder, blueberries, chocolate chips, and bananas.

2. In a separate cup, whisk together the eggs, vanilla extract, and butter.

3. Preheat your air fryer to 320°F, spray it with cooking spray, and add some oats to the bottom.

4. Pour in the egg and cinnamon mixture, stir well, and cook for about 20 minutes.

5. Combine again, divide into cups, and serve with tea. Have fun!

13. Ham Breakfast

Preparation time: 13 minutes

Cooking time: 20 minutes

Servings: 8

Ingredients

- Spray for cooking

- Season with black pepper and salt

- 2 tablespoons Mustard

- 8 eggs

- 3 quarts milk

- 6 oz. shredded cheddar cheese

- 12 ounces cubed ham

- 6 oz. chopped green chilies

- 8 cups cubed French bread

Instructions:

1. Spray the air fryer with cooking spray and preheat it to 350 degrees Fahrenheit

2. In a mixing bowl, whisk together the cheese, milk, salt, mustard, and pepper with the eggs.

3. Put the bread cubes in an air fryer and toss with the ham and chilies.

4. Pour in the egg mixture, spread evenly, and cook for about 15 minutes.

5. Cut in half and divide among plates. Have fun!

14. Yummy Breakfast Soufflé

Time to prepare: 15 minutes

Cooking time: 10 minutes

Servings: 5

Ingredients

- 3 tablespoons chopped chives

- 3 tablespoons chopped parsley

- a pinch of crushed red chili pepper

- Heavy cream, 5 tablespoons.

- 5 whisked eggs

- Season with salt and black pepper

Instructions

1. In a large pot, whisk together the salt, eggs, heavy cream, pepper, red chili pepper, chives, and parsley. Divide the mixture into four soufflé bowls.

2. Arrange the pots in your air fryer and bake the soufflés for 8 minutes at 350 degrees F.

3. Warm them up before serving. Also, have fun!

15. Egg Bowls for Breakfast

Time to prepare: 15 minutes

Cooking time: 25 minutes

Servings:5

Ingredients

- 5 teaspoons grated parmesan

- Season with black pepper and salt

- 5 teaspoons parsley and chives (mixed)

- a dozen eggs

- Heavy cream, 5 tablespoons

- 5 dinner rolls, with the tops cut off and the insides, scooped out

Instructions:

1. Put your dinner rolls on a baking tray and crack an egg into each one.

2. Toss the heavy cream with the mixed herbs in each roll and season with pepper and salt.

3. Sprinkle some parmesan cheese on top of the rolls, place them in your air fryer, and cook for about 25 minutes at 350°F.

4. Arrange the bread bowls on plates and serve them as breakfast. Also, have fun!

16. Breakfast with Tomatoes and Bacon

Time to prepare: 12 minutes

Cooking time: 35 minutes

Servings: 8

Ingredients

- 2-pound cubed white bread

- 2 pounds cooked and chopped smoked bacon

- 14 cup extra virgin olive oil

- 2 chopped yellow onions

- 30 ounces chopped canned tomatoes

- 1 teaspoon crushed red pepper

- 1-pound shredded cheddar

- 3 tablespoons chopped chives

- 1-pound shredded Monterey jack cheese

- 3 tablespoons chicken reserve

- Season with salt and black pepper

- 10 whisked eggs

Instructions:

1. Pour some oil into your air fryer and heat it to 350 degrees F.

2. Combine the bacon, bread, tomatoes, onion, red pepper, and stock in a large mixing bowl.

3. Combine the cheddar, eggs, and Monterey jack cheeses in a saucepan and cook for about 20 minutes.

4. Divide into bowls and top with chives before serving. Have fun!

17.Yummy Breakfast Potatoes

Time to prepare: 15 minutes

Cooking time: 40 minutes

Servings: 5

Ingredients

- 2 teaspoon powdered onion

- 2 teaspoons paprika (sweet)

- 2 teaspoon powdered garlic

- Season with black pepper and salt

- 2 chopped red bell peppers

- 2 chopped yellow onions

- 4 cubed potatoes

- 3 tablespoons of extra virgin olive oil

Instructions:

1. Drizzle some olive oil into your air fryer basket, add your potatoes, toss, and season with pepper and salt.

2. Toss in the garlic powder, onion, paprika, bell pepper, and onion powder, stir well, cover, and cook for 30 minutes at 370 degrees F.

3. For lunch, divide the mixed potatoes into bowls and eat them. Have fun!

18. Polenta Bites

Time to prepare: 12 minutes

Cooking time: 25 minutes

Servings: 6

Ingredients

To make the polenta, combine the following ingredients in a mixing bowl.

- 4 quarts water

- 1 pound cornmeal

- 2 tablespoons melted butter

- Season with black pepper and salt

For the polenta bites, prepare as follows:

- Spray for cooking

- 2 tablespoons of sugar

Instructions:

1. In a saucepan, whisk together the butter, cornmeal, pepper, and salt

2. Bring to a boil over medium-high heat, then reduce to low heat and steam for around 10 minutes. Remove from heat, stir well, and chill until cold

3. Scoop a tablespoon of polenta onto a work surface and roll into a sphere

4. Repeat with the remaining polenta; put all of the balls in the cooking basket of your air fryer, spray with cooking spray, cover, and cook for about 8 minutes at 380 degrees F.

5. Arrange polenta bites in cups, sprinkle with sugar, and serve for brunch

19.Muffins with Eggs

Time to prepare: 12 minutes

Time to cook: 18 minutes

Servings: 5

Ingredients

- Worcestershire sauce (optional)

- 3 eggs

- 3 oz. grated parmesan

- 2 teaspoons baking powder

- 4.5 oz of white flour

- 4-5 tablespoons of milk

- 3 tablespoon of extra virgin olive oil

Instructions

1. In a mixing bowl, whisk together the egg, oil, flour, milk, baking powder, parmesan, and Worcestershire, divided into 5 silicone muffin cups.

2. Arrange the cups in the air fryer's baking basket, cover, and steam for 15 minutes at 392 degrees F.

3. Serve warmly for brunch. Have fun!

20. Breakfast in a Rustic Style

Time to prepare: 12 minutes

Time to prepare: 15 minutes

Servings: 5

Ingredients

- Spray for cooking

- a dozen eggs

- 5 chopped bacon slices

- 5 chipolatas and 2 minced garlic cloves

- Season with black pepper and salt

- 10 halved tomatoes

- 10 halved chestnut mushrooms

- 8 oz, baby spinach

Instructions

1. Melt some butter or oil in a pan and add some garlic, onions, and basil, and mushrooms to your pan of cooking

2. Add the chipolatas and bacon, then the spinach and broken eggs.

3. Season with pepper and salt, then place your pan in the air fryer's cooking basket and bake for about 15 minutes at 350 degrees F.

4. Serve them for breakfast by dividing them into bowls. Have fun!

21. Air fried Sandwich

Time to prepare: 15 minutes

Time to cook: 8 minutes

Servings: 4

Ingredients

- 3 halved English muffins

- 3 eggs

- 3 strips of bacon

- Season with black pepper and salt

Instructions

1. Break and add the eggs to your air fryer, top with bacon, cover, and cook for around 6 minutes at 392 degrees F

2. Warm your English muffin halves in the oven for a few seconds, then break the eggs into two halves, top with bacon, season with salt and pepper, and top with the other half of your English muffins

22. Delicious Cinnamon Toast

Time to prepare: 13 minutes

Time to cook: 8 minutes

Servings:8

Ingredients

- 2 and 12 teaspoons powdered cinnamon

- 2 teaspoons of vanilla extract

- 1 pound of sugar

- 16 slices of bread

- 2 soft butter sticks

Instructions

1. In a mixing bowl, combine the soft butter, vanilla, sugar, and cinnamon and stir well.

2. Spread this on your bread slices, place them in the air fryer, and cook for 5 minutes at 400°F.

3. Serve them for brunch by dividing them into plates. Have fun!

Chapter-3: Air Fryer Appetizer Recipes

1.Pumpkin Muffins

Time to prepare: 15 minutes

Cooking time: 20 minutes

Servings:20

Ingredients

- 1 teaspoon powdered baking soda

- 2 eggs

- 1 teaspoon bicarbonate of soda

- 2 teaspoon ground cinnamon

- 1 teaspoon ground nutmeg

- 1 pound of sugar

- 12 cups of flour

- flaxseed meal (four tablespoons)

- 1 cup pureed pumpkin

- 12 cup melted butter

Instructions:

1. In a small mixing bowl, thoroughly combine the butter, pumpkin puree, and egg.

2. Blend flour, flaxseed meal, nutmeg, baking soda, sugar, baking powder, and cinnamon in a large mixing bowl.

3. Preheat the oven to 350 degrees F and bake the muffins for 15 minutes in a muffin pan that suits your fryer.

4. Serve the muffins cold as a snack. Have fun!

2.Pesto Crackers

Time to prepare: 15 minutes

Cooking time: 20 minutes

Servings:5

Ingredients

- 4 teaspoons unsalted butter

- 4 tablespoon pesto (basil)

- 2 minced garlic cloves

- half teaspoon of dried basil

- a cup and a half of flour

- Season with salt and black pepper

- 1 teaspoon powdered baking soda

Instructions:

1. In a mixing bowl, mix the pepper, salt, flour, baking powder, cayenne, garlic, pesto, basil, and butter until the dough is firm.

2. Place the dough on a lined baking sheet that suits your air fryer, set the temperature to about 325 degrees F, and bake for 17 minutes.

3. Allow cooling before breaking and eating crackers as a snack or lunch. Have fun!

3.Cauliflower Bars

Time to prepare: 15 minutes

Cooking time: 30 minutes

Servings: 15

Ingredients

- Season with salt and black pepper

- 2 teaspoon seasoning (Italian)

- 1 egg white

- 1 cup shredded mozzarella

- 2 large cauliflower heads, divided florets

Instructions

1. Put cauliflower florets in a food mixer and process until smooth. Spread on a lined baking sheet that matches your air fryer, place in the fryer, and cook for about 10 minutes at 360 degrees F.

2. Transfer cauliflower to a small bowl, add pepper, salt, egg whites, cheese, and Italian seasoning, stir well, and scatter into a rectangular pan that fits your air fryer, pressing well. Put in the fryer and cook for another 15 minutes at 360°F.

3. Cut into 12-15 bars, place on a tray, and serve. Have fun!

4.Zucchini Cakes

Time to prepare: 15 minutes

Cooking time:15 minutes

Servings: 5

Ingredients

- 4 grated zucchinis

- 4 minced garlic cloves

- 2 chopped yellow onions

- Season with black pepper and salt

- 1 cup flour (whole wheat)

- 2 eggs

- 1 cup chopped dill

- Spray for cooking

Instructions:

1. In a small bowl, combine zucchini, onion, garlic, salt, flour, egg, pepper, and dill; stir well. Shape small patties from this mixture; spray with cooking spray; place in the tray of your air fryer; and cook for around 6 minutes on each side at 370 degrees F.

2. Serve them as a snack right away. Have fun!

5.Shrimp Muffins

Time to prepare: 15 minutes

Cooking Time: 30 minutes

Servings: 8

Ingredients

- Spray for cooking

- Season with black pepper and salt

- 2 minced garlic cloves

- 2 teaspoon flakes of parsley

- 2 & 12 cup panko

- 10 ounces peeled, fried, and chopped shrimp

- 2 cup shredded mozzarella

- 4 tablespoons of mayonnaise

- 2 peeled and halved spaghetti squash

Instructions:

1. Place the squash halves in your air fryer and cook for 16 minutes at 350 degrees F. Remove the squash halves from the air fryer and grate the flesh into a small bowl.

2. Combine the pepper, salt, panko, parsley flakes, mayonnaise, lobster, and mozzarella in a large mixing bowl.

3. Spray a muffin tray that fits your air fryer with cooking spray and divide the squash and shrimp mixture into each cup.

4. Place them in the fryer and cook them for about 10 minutes at 360°F.

5. Place the muffins on a platter and serve as a snack. Have fun!

6.Apple Snack from Mexico

Time to prepare: 15 minutes

Cooking time: 10 minutes

Servings: 5

Ingredients

- 1 cup caramel sauce (clean)
- 1 cup chocolate chips (dark)
- 12 cup chopped pecans
- 1 tablespoon lemon juice
- 6 broad apples, peeled, cored, and cubed

Instructions

1. In a small bowl, combine the apples and lemon juice, stir well, and transfer to an air fryer-safe pan.

2. Throw in the pecans and chocolate chips, drizzle with caramel sauce, blend well, and put in the fryer to steam for around 5 minutes at 320°F.

3. Gently rotate, break into small bowls, and serve immediately as a snack. Have fun!

7.Potato Compote

Time to prepare: 15 minutes

Cooking time: 15 minutes

Servings: 15

Ingredients

- White pepper and a pinch of salt

- 4 tablespoons of Water

- 1 teaspoon cumin powder

- 6 minced garlic cloves

- 3 tablespoons extra virgin olive oil

- 4 tablespoon lemon juice

- 12 cup tahini

- 2 cups peeled and chopped sweet potatoes

- 20 ounces drained canned garbanzo beans

Instructions

1. Put the potatoes in the basket of your air fryer and cook for 15 minutes at 360 degrees F. Cool them down, peel them, and place them in your food processor. Pitching, bowling

2. Combine the sesame paste, ginger, beans, lemon juice, cumin, water, and oil in a mixing bowl.

3. Season with salt and black pepper, then divide and serve in small bowls. Have fun!

8. Banana Snack

Time to prepare: 15 minutes

Cooking time: 10 minutes

Servings: 10

Ingredients

- 2 teaspoon vegetable oil

- 2 peeled and sliced bananas (16 bits each)

- 1 cup cocoa powder

- 1 pound peanut butter

- Crust for 18 baking cups

Instructions

1. Put the chocolate chips in a small jar, heat over medium heat, stir until the chocolate melts and remove from the heat.

2. In a cup, combine the peanut butter and coconut oil and stir well.

3. Place 1 teaspoon of chocolate mix, 1 slice of banana, and 1 teaspoon of butter mix in a cup.

4. Repeat with the remaining cups, placing them all in a dish that suits your air fryer, frying for around 5 minutes at about 320 degrees F, then switching to the refrigerator until ready to serve as a snack. Have fun!

9.Snack of Buffalo Cauliflower

Time to prepare: 15 minutes

Cooking time: 20 minutes

Servings: 5

Ingredients

- 1 tablespoon buffalo sauce

- 1/2 cup melted butter

- 2 cups bread crumbs (panko)

- 6 cups florets de cauliflower

- For serving, mayonnaise

Instructions

1. In a small bowl, whisk together the buffalo sauce and butter.

2. Throw the cauliflower florets in the mixture and roll them in panko bread crumbs.

3. Place them in the basket of your air fryer and cook for 15 minutes at 350 degrees Fahrenheit.

4. Place them on a platter and serve with mayonnaise on the side. Have fun!

10. Coconut Chicken Bites

Time to prepare: 15 minutes

Cooking time: 15 minutes

Servings: 5

Ingredients

- 10 pieces of chicken tenders
- Spray for cooking
- 1 cup shredded coconut
- 1 cup bread crumbs (panko)
- Season with black pepper and salt
- 3 eggs
- 4 teaspoons garlic powder

Instructions

1. In a small cup, whisk together the eggs, pepper, salt, and garlic powder.

2. In a separate cup, mix the coconut and panko and stir well.

3. Dip the chicken wings in an egg mixture before coating one well in coconut.

4. Coat the chicken bites with cooking spray, place them in the air fryer basket, and cook for about 10 minutes at 350 degrees F.

5. Plance them on a platter to serve as an appetizer. Have fun!

11.Bread Sticks

Time to prepare: 15 minutes

Cooking time: 15 minutes

Servings:5

Ingredients

- a smidgeon of nutmeg

- 1-pound brown sugar

- 2 tablespoons of honey

- 2 teaspoon ground cinnamon

- A half-cup of milk

- 3 eggs

- 6 slices of bread, each cut into 6 sticks

Instructions

1. In a mixing bowl, add the eggs, brown sugar, milk, nutmeg, cinnamon, and honey.

2. Dip your breadsticks in the mixture, place them in the basket of your air fryer, and cook for about 10 minutes at 360°F.

3. To use as snacks, break the breadsticks into dishes. Have fun!

12.Chips made from apples

Time to prepare: 15 minutes

Cooking time: 15 minutes

Servings: 4

Ingredients

- 2 teaspoons white sugar

- 1 teaspoon powdered cinnamon

- a grain of salt

- 2 cored and sliced apples

Instructions

1. In a pot, combine the salt, apple slices, sugar, and cinnamon; stir well. Transfer to your air fryer's basket and cook for about 10 minutes at 390 degrees F, turning once.

2. To act as a party snack, cut the bowls of apple chips in half. Have fun!

13. Sweet Popcorn

Time to prepare: 10 minutes

Cooking time: 15 minutes

Servings: 6

Ingredients

- 3 tablespoon brown sugar

- 3 and 12 tablespoons butter

- 4 tablespoons corn kernels

Instructions

1. Put the corn kernels in the air fryer pan and cook for about 6 minutes at 400 degrees F. Transfer to a serving dish, scatter, and set aside for now.

2. Melt the butter on a plate over low heat, then add the sugar and stir until it is fully dissolved.

3. Toss in the popcorn, flip to completely cover, remove from the heat, and scatter on the plate once more.

4. Refrigerate until ready to eat, then divide into bowls and serve as a snack or lunch. Have fun!

14. Chicken Dip

Time to prepare: 15 minutes

Cooking time: 30 minutes

Servings: 12

Ingredients

- 1 tablespoon chutney

- Season with black pepper and salt

- 1 cup sliced almonds

- 12 cup chopped cilantro

- a third cup of raisins

- 8 oz. of grated Monterey jack cheese

- 6 chopped scallions

- 1 tablespoon curry powder

- 3 cups cooked and shredded chicken meat

- 14 oz of Cream cheese

- 2 cup plain yogurt

- 4 tablespoons melted butter

Instructions

1. In a mixing bowl, combine the cream cheese and milk and beat with an electric mixer until smooth.

2. Add the scallions, curry powder, raisins, cheese, chicken meat, salt, cilantro, and pepper, and stir to mix.

3. Place in an air fryer baking dish, scatter almonds on top, bake for 25 minutes at about 300 degrees, break into serving dishes, top with chutney, and serve as an appetizer. Have fun!

15.Sausage Balls

Time to prepare: 15 minutes

Cooking time: 20 minutes

Servings: 10

Ingredients

- 4 tablespoon breadcrumbs
- 2 chopped small onions
- 1 teaspoon minced garlic
- 2 tablespoon sage
- Season with black pepper and salt
- 6 oz. ground sausage meat

Instructions

1. In a pot, combine the sausage, pepper, salt, onion, sage, garlic, breadcrumbs, and mix well. Shape the mixture into small balls.

2. Place them in the air fryer basket, cook for 15 minutes at 360 degrees F, break into batches and serve as a snack. Have fun!

16.Snack on chickpeas

Time to prepare: 12 minutes

Cooking time: 12 minutes

Servings: 6

Ingredients

- Season with a pinch of salt and black pepper to taste.

- 2 teaspoons of paprika (smoked)

- 2 tablespoons extra virgin olive oil

- 1 teaspoon cumin powder

- 17 ounces drained canned chickpeas

Instructions

1. Toss the chickpeas with the cumin, oil, salt, paprika, and pepper in a pan to coat, then move to the fryer basket and cook for about 10 minutes at 390°F.

2. Cut into small bowls and serve as a snack. Have fun!

17.Dill Pickles Fried in the Cold

Time to prepare: 15 minutes

Cooking time: 10 minutes

Servings: 6

Ingredients

- 12 cup ranch dressing

- Spray for cooking

- 1 teaspoon paprika (sweet)

- 1 teaspoon powdered garlic

- 12 cups of milk

- 2 eggs

- 1 cup all-purpose flour

- 18 ounces dill pickles in bowls, split into wedges, and pat dry

Instructions

1. In a mixing bowl, whisk together the milk and the egg.

2. In a separate cup, whisk together the flour, garlic powder, salt, and paprika.

3. Dip the pickles in flour, then in the egg mixture, and then back in flour before putting them in the air fryer.

4. Coat pickle wedges in cooking oil, cook for 5 minutes at 400 degrees F, transfer to a bowl, and serve with ranch sauce on the side. Have fun!

18.Crab Sticks

Time to prepare: 15 minutes

Cooking time:15 minutes

Servings: 5

Ingredients

- 5 teaspoons of Cajun seasoning

- 4 tablespoons of sesame seed oil

- 12 halved crabsticks

Instructions

1. Throw the crab sticks in a pot with some sesame oil and Cajun seasoning, toss to blend, switch to the basket of your air fryer, and cook for 12 minutes at 350°F.

2. Arrange on a platter as an appetizer. Have fun!

19.Crispy Radish Chips

Time to prepare: 15 minutes

Cooking time:15 minutes

Servings: 5

Ingredients

- 2 tablespoons chopped chives

- Season with black pepper and salt

- 18 sliced radishes

- Spray for cooking

Instructions

1. Arrange radish slices in the basket of your air fryer, brush with cooking oil, season with salt and black pepper to taste, and cook for around 10 minutes at 350 degrees F, turning halfway.

2. Transfer to bowls and serve with chives sprinkled on top. Have fun!

20.Spring Rolls

Time to prepare: 15 minutes

Cooking time: 30 minutes

Servings: 10

Ingredients

- 4 tablespoons of water

- 4 tablespoons of cornflour

- 12 sheets of spring rolls

- 4 tablespoons of extra virgin olive oil

- 2 tablespoon soy sauce

- Season with salt and black pepper

- 4 minced garlic cloves

- 2 tablespoon grated ginger

- 2 teaspoons of sugar

- 1 minced chili pepper

- 2 grated carrots

- 4 chopped yellow onions

- 4 cups shredded green cabbage

Instructions

1. Heat the oil in a skillet over medium-high heat, then add the cabbage, carrots, onions, ginger, chili pepper, sugar, garlic, pepper, salt, and soy sauce, and mix well. Cook for around 2-3 minutes, then remove from the heat and set aside to cool.

2. Cut each spring roll sheet into a circle with a cabbage mix, then transform them.

3. In a jar, combine the cornflour and water, whisk well, and use this paste to seal the spring rolls.

4. Place the spring rolls in the air fryer basket and cook for around 10 minutes at 360°F.

5. Flip the roll and cook for an additional 10 minutes.

6. Place them on a platter and act as an appetizer. Have fun!

21. Banana Chips

Time to prepare: 15 minutes

Cooking time: 20 minutes

Servings: 5

Ingredients

- 2 teaspoons extra virgin olive oil

- 1 teaspoon masala chat

- 1 teaspoon powdered turmeric

- a grain of salt

- 6 peeled and cut bananas

Instructions

1. In a small bowl, combine banana slices, turmeric, salt, chat masala, and oil; mix well and set aside for around 10 minutes.

2. Put banana slices in your preheated air fryer at about 360 degrees F and cook for around 15 minutes, rotating once.

3. Serve as a light snack. Have fun!

22. Salmon Party Patties

Time to prepare: 15 minutes

Cooking time: 30 minutes

Servings: 6

Ingredients

- Spray for cooking

- 4 tablespoons of breadcrumbs

- 2 eggs

- Season with salt and black pepper

- 4 tablespoon chopped dill

- 4 tablespoons chopped parsley

- 2 large skinless, boneless salmon fillets

- 6 large boiled, drained, and mashed potatoes

Instructions

1. Put your salmon in the basket of your air fryer and cook for 10 minutes at 360 degrees F.

2. Move the salmon to a cutting board, set it aside to cool, then flake it in a jar.

3. Combine salt, mashed potatoes, dill, pepper, egg, parsley, and bread crumbs in a mixing bowl and mix well. Form eight or more patties.

4. Put the salmon patties in the basket of your air fryer, spray with cooking oil, and cook for 12 minutes at 360

degrees F, rotating halfway through. Transfer to a serving dish and serve as an appetizer. Have fun!

23.Honey Party Wings

Time to prepare: 1 hour and 30 minutes

Cooking time :15 minutes

Servings:8

Ingredients

- 4 tablespoons of lime juice

- Season with black pepper and salt

- tablespoons of honey

- 4 tablespoons of Soy sauce

- 20 halved chicken wings

Instructions

1. In a small bowl, combine the chicken wings, honey, soy sauce, pepper, salt, and lime juice; stir well and chill for 1 hour.

2. Move the chicken wings to the air fryer and cook for 12 minutes at 360 degrees F, turning halfway through.

3. Place them on a platter to serve as an appetizer. Have fun!

24.Snack of Beef Jerky

Time to prepare: 2 hours and 30 minutes

Cooking time:1 hour and 40 minutes

Servings:8

Ingredients

- 4-pound sliced beef round

- 4 tablespoons of cayenne pepper

- 4 tablespoon black peppercorns

- 1 tablespoon of Worcestershire sauce

- 4 cups of Soy sauce

Instructions:

1. In a small bowl, whisk together black pepper, black peppercorns, and Worcestershire sauce with soy sauce.

2. Add the beef slices, toss to coat, and put in the refrigerator for around 6 hours.

3. Put the beef rounds in the fryer and cook for 1 hour and 30 minutes at 370 degrees F.

4. In a container, shift and eat cold. Have fun!

25.Zucchini Chips

Time to prepare: 15 minutes

Cooking time: 1 hour and 20 minutes

Servings: 8

Ingredients

- 4 tablespoons of extra virgin olive oil

- 4 tablespoons of balsamic vinaigrette

- Season with salt and black pepper

- 6 thinly sliced zucchinis

Instructions

1. In a small cup, whisk together the salt, vinegar, oil, and pepper.

2. Throw the zucchini slices in the batter, coat well, and cook for 1 hour at 200 degrees F in your air fryer.

3. Serve cold zucchini chips as a snack. Have fun!

Chapter-4: Dessert Recipes

1.Grapefruit, broiled in the air fryer

Preparation: 10 minutes

Cooking time: 16 minutes

Servings: 2

Ingredients

- 1 refrigerated red grapefruit

- 1 tablespoon butter that has been softened

- 1 tablespoon Brown sugar is a type of sugar that is used

- 2 tablespoon Brown sugar is a type of sugar that is used

- Foil made of aluminum

- 12 teaspoon Cinnamon powder

Instructions

1. Preheat the air fryer to 200 degrees Celsius / 400 degrees Fahrenheit

2. If the grapefruit isn't sitting flat, cut it in half crosswise and slice a thin sliver off the bottom of each half. To make the grapefruit easier to eat until cooked, cut around the outside edge and between each segment with a sharp paring knife.

3. 1 tablespoon of softened butter, 1 tablespoon of a small bowl of brown sugar Apply the mixture to each half of a grapefruit. The remaining brown sugar should be sprinkled on top.

4. Cut two 5-inch squares of aluminum foil and put each grapefruit half on one; fold up the edges to capture any juices. Place in the air fryer basket.

5. 6–7 minutes in the air fryer before the sugar mixture is bubbling. Until serving, sprinkle the fruit with cinnamon.

2. Apples with Brown Sugar and Pecans Roasted in the Air Fryer

Time to prepare: 10minutes

Cooking time: 20 minutes

Servings: 2

Ingredients

- 2 tablespoons pecans, coarsely chopped

- 1 tablespoons sugar (brown)

- 1 tablespoon flour (all-purpose)

- 14 tablespoon apple pie seasoning

- 2 medium apples, peeled and cored, cut into wedges

- 1 tablespoon melted butter

Instructions

1. Preheat the air fryer to 360 degrees Fahrenheit (180 degrees Celsius) (180 degrees C).

2. In a small mixing bowl, add pecans, brown sugar, flour, and apple pie spice. In a medium mixing bowl, toss apple wedges with butter and toss to cover. In the air fryer basket, arrange the apples in a single layer and top with the pecan mixture.

3. Cook for 10 to 15 minutes in a preheated air fryer until apples are tender.

Note from the Chef:

Apple pie spice can be substituted with cinnamon.

3.Cinnamon-Sugar Doughnuts in the Air Fryer

Preparation time: 10 minutes

Cooking time:10 minutes

Servings:8

Ingredients:

- 14 cup melted butter

- 12 cup sugar (white)

- a quarter cup of brown sugar

- 1 tablespoon cinnamon powder

- 14 teaspoon nutmeg powder (Optional)

- 16.3 ounces package flaky biscuit dough refrigerated

Instructions

1. In a mixing bowl, melt the butter. In a separate cup, add white sugar, brown sugar, cinnamon, and nutmeg.

2. Distribute the biscuit dough into separate biscuits and cut out the centers with a biscuit cutter to create a

doughnut shape (or the bottom of a piping tip). Place the doughnuts in the air fryer basket.

3. 4 to 6 minutes at 350 degrees F (175 degrees C) before golden brown. Cook for 1 to 3 more minutes after flipping the doughnuts.

4. Take the doughnuts out of the air fryer. A dip of doughnut in melted butter (ensuring that the top, bottom, and sides are all covered), then in the sugar-cinnamon mixture until completely coated. Serve right away.

Note from the Chef:

Microwave doughnuts for 8 to 10 seconds to reheat, only long enough to soften them up again.

4.Roasted Bananas in the Air Fryer

Preparation time: 2 minutes

Cooking time: 7 minutes

Servings: 1

Ingredients

- 1 banana, sliced diagonally in 1/8" thick slices

- avocado oil(for cooking spray)

Instructions

1. Using parchment paper, line the air fryer basket.

2. Preheat your air fryer to 375°F (190 degrees C).

3. Place banana slices in the basket, making sure they don't touch; if possible, cook in batches. Avocado oil should be sprayed on banana slices.

4. Cook for 5 minutes in the air fryer. Remove the banana slices from the basket and carefully flip them (they will be soft). Cook for another 2 to 3 minutes, or until the banana slices are browning and caramelized. Remove from the basket with care.

5.Churros cooked in an air fryer

Preparation time:5 minutes

Cooking:15-minute timer

Time: 25 minutes

Servings: 6

Ingredients

- 14 cup butter

- 12 cup milk

- 1 teaspoon of salt

- 12 cup flour (all-purpose)

- 2 eggs

- a quarter cup of white sugar

- 12 teaspoon of Cinnamon powder

Instructions

1. In a saucepan over medium-high heat, melt the butter. Pour in the milk and season with salt. Reduce heat to medium and bring to a boil, constantly stirring with a wooden spoon. Put the flour all at once. Stir the dough before it comes together.

2. Remove from the heat and set aside for 5 to 7 minutes to cool. With a wooden spoon, mix in the eggs before the pastry comes together. Fill a pastry bag with the dough and a big star tip right into the air fryer basket, pipe dough into strips.

3. Air fried churros for 5 minutes at 340 degrees F (175 degrees C).

4. Meanwhile, in a small cup, mix the sugar and cinnamon and pour onto a shallow plate.

5. Take the fried churros out of the air fryer and roll them in the cinnamon-sugar mix.

6. Apple Pies in the Air Fryer

Preparation time:30minutes

Cooking time:15-minute timer

Servings:4

Ingredients:

- 4 tablespoons a stick of butter

- 6 tablespoons Brown sugar is a type of sugar that is used

- 1 tablespoon Cinnamon powder

- 2 medium diced granny smith apples

- 1 tablespoon Cornstarch is a thickening agent.

- 2 tablespoon Water that is ice cold

- For a 9-inch double-crust pie, 12 (14 ounces) box pastry

- Spray for cooking

- 12 tablespoons made from grapeseed's

- a quarter cup of powdered sugar

- 1 tablespoon a glass of milk

Instructions

1. In a nonstick skillet, combine the apples, butter, brown sugar, and cinnamon. Cook for 5 minutes over medium heat or until apples have softened.

2. Cornstarch should be dissolved in cold water. Cook, constantly stirring, until the sauce thickens, around 1 minute. As you prepare the crust, remove the apple pie filling from the heat and set it aside to cool.

3. Unroll the pie crust on a lightly floured surface and gently roll it out to smooth the surface. Cut the dough into rectangles that will fit into your air fryer two at a time. Continue with the remaining crust until you have 8 equal rectangles, re-rolling scraps of dough as required.

4. Wet the outer edges of four rectangles with water and fill the middle with apple filling about 1/2-inch from the edges. Roll out the remaining four rectangles slightly larger than the filled rectangles. Place these rectangles on top of the filling and use a fork to seal the edges. Cut four narrow slits in the pies' tops.

5. Using cooking oil, coat the air fryer basket. Using a spatula, brush the tops of two pies with grapeseed oil and move them to the air fryer basket.

6. Place the basket in the oven and preheat an air fryer to 350 degrees F (175 degrees C). Bake for about 8 minutes, or until golden brown. Remove the pies from the basket and repeat the process with the remaining two pies.

7. In a small cup, combine powdered sugar and milk. Enable to dry after brushing glaze on warm pies. Warm or room temperature pies may be served.

7. Oreos in the Air Fryer

Preparation time: 5 minutes

Cooking time: 5 minutes

Servings:9

Ingredients:

- 12 cup full pancake maker

- a third of a cup of water

- Spray for cooking

- 9 cookies with chocolate sandwich filling

- 1 tablespoon Sugar for confectioners

Instructions

1. Combine the pancake mix and water in a large mixing bowl.

2. Using parchment paper, line an air fryer basket. Using nonstick cooking spray, coat parchment paper. Place each cookie in the basket after dipping it in the pancake batter. Make sure they're not touching and, if possible, cook them in batches.

3. Preheat the air fryer to 200 degrees Celsius (200 degrees C) / 400 degrees Fahrenheit Cook for 4 to 5 minutes with the basket in place; flip and cook for another 2 to 3 minutes. Confectioners' sugar can be sprinkled on top.

8.Triple-Chocolate Oatmeal Cookies in the Air Fryer

Preparation time:15-minute timer

Cooking time: 10 minutes

Servings: 36

Ingredients

- 3 cups oatmeal (quick-cooking)
- 12 cup flour (all-purpose)
- a quarter cup of cocoa powder
- 3.4 oz of chocolate pudding mix
- 1 tablespoon Soda (baking)
- 1 tablespoon sodium chloride
- 1 cup softened butter
- a third of a cup of brown sugar
- a third of a cup of white sugar
- 2 eggs
- 1 tablespoon of Extract of vanilla
- 2cup of chocolate chippings
- 1 cup walnuts, chopped (optional)
- nonstick cooking spray

Instructions

- Preheat an air fryer to 350 degrees F (175 degrees C), as

instructed by the manufacturer. Using nonstick cooking spray, coat the air fryer basket.

- Combine the oatmeal, flour, pudding mix, baking soda, and salt in a mixing bowl. Remove from the equation.

- Using an electric mixer, cream together butter, brown sugar, and white sugar in a separate bowl. Combine the eggs and vanilla extract in a mixing bowl. Mix in the oatmeal mixture thoroughly. Combine the chocolate chips and walnuts in a mixing bowl.

- Using a large cookie scoop, drop dough into the air fryer; flatten out and leave about 1 inch between each cookie.

- Cook for 6 to 10 minutes, or until lightly browned. Until serving, cool on a wire rack.

Notes from the Chef

- Omit the cocoa powder and substitute the chocolate pudding mix with vanilla pudding mix for a traditional oatmeal-chocolate chip cookie. Even half the recipe saves the instant pudding for another time while making these cookies.

- Cookies took just 8 minutes to bake. Start testing at 6 minutes because every air fryer is different. Cook for 1 to 3 more minutes for crispier cookies.

- You can use any kind of nut you like.

9.Banana Cake with Air Fryer

Preparation time:10 minutes

Cooking time: 30 minutes

Servings:4

Ingredients:

- Spray for cooking

- a third of a cup of brown sugar

- 12 tablespoons of space temperature butter

- 1 mashed banana

- 1 egg

- 2 tablespoon Honeydew nectarines

- 1 cup flour (self-rising)

- 12 teaspoons of Cinnamon powder

- 1 teaspoon of salt

Instructions

1. Preheat your air fryer to 160 degrees C / 320°F. Using cooking spray, coat a small fluted tube pan.

2. Using an electric mixer, cream together the sugar and butter in a mixing bowl. In a separate cup, combine the banana, egg, and honey. Blend the banana mixture into the butter mixture until it is fully smooth.

3. Combine the flour, cinnamon, and salt in a sifter and sift into the banana-butter mixture. Blend the batter until it is smooth. Transfer to the prepared pan and use the back of a spoon to level the surface.

4. In the air fryer basket, position the cake pan. Set the timer for 30 minutes after sliding the basket into the air fryer. It is cooked when inserting a toothpick into the center of the cake comes out clean.

10.Butter Cake that has been air-fried

Preparation time: 10 minutes

Cooking: 15-minute timer

Servings:4

Ingredients

- Spray for cooking
- 7 tablespoons space temperature butter
- a quarter cup of white sugar
- 2 tablespoon granulated sugar
- 1 egg
- 1 and a half cups all-purpose flour
- 1 teaspoon of salt
- 6 tablespoons a bottle of milk

Instructions

- Preheat your air fryer to 350°F (180 degrees C). Using cooking spray, coat a small fluted tube pan.

- 1/4 cup plus 2 tablespoons of butter, creamed Using an electric mixer, beat the butter and sugar together in a mixing bowl until light and fluffy. Mix in the egg until it is smooth and fluffy. Combine flour and salt in a mixing dish. Add the milk and thoroughly blend the batter. Move the batter to the prepared pan and smooth the top with the back of a spoon.

- In the air fryer basket, place the pan. Make a 15-minute timer. Cook until a toothpick inserted into the center of the cake comes out clean.

- Remove the cake from the pan and set it aside to cool for 5 minutes.

11.Inventive+ phrasing Apple Pies in the Air Fryer

Preparation time:15-minute timer

Cooking time: 10 minutes

Servings:10

Ingredients:

- (14.1 ounces) 1 box refrigerated pie crusts

- (21 ounces)1 can apple pie filling

- 1 beaten egg

- 2 tablespoon sugar and cinnamon

- cooking spray

Instructions

1. Roll out 1 pie crust on a lightly floured surface with a rolling pin. Break the pie crust into 10 circles with a 2-1/4-inch round biscuit or cookie cutter. Create a total of 20 pie crust circles by repeating the procedure with the second pie crust.

2. Half of each circle should be filled with apple pie filling. Make a mini pie by placing a second pie crust circle on top. Do not overfill the container. To seal the mini pies, press down the edges and crimp with a fork. Brush the tops of the muffins with beaten egg and cinnamon sugar.

3. Preheat the air fryer to 360 degrees Fahrenheit (180 degrees Celsius) (175 degrees C).

4. Gently coat the air fryer basket in cooking oil. Place a batch of mini pies in the air fryer basket, leaving enough room around each one for air to circulate.

5. Bake for 5 to 7 minutes, or until golden brown. Remove the pies from the basket and finish baking the remaining pies. Warm or at room temperature is fine.

Observations

- If you have big apple slices, split them in half before filling the mini pies.

- Other fruit pie fillings can be used in this recipe as well.

12.Donut Sticks from the Air Fryer

Preparation time: 20 minutes

Cooking time:15-minute timer

Servings:8

Ingredients

- 1 box refrigerated crescent roll dough (8 ounces)

- 14 cup melted butter

- 12 cup sugar (white)

- 2 tablespoon cinnamon powder

- 12 cup fruit jam (any flavor)

Instructions

1. Roll out the crescent roll dough sheet to an 8x12-inch rectangle. Break the dough in half lengthwise and crosswise into 1/2-inch thick "sticks" with a pizza cutter. Dip doughnut sticks in melted butter and put in a single layer in the air fryer basket.

2. Cook for 4 to 5 minutes in an air fryer at 380 degrees F (195 degrees C) until well browned.

3. In a pie plate or shallow dish, combine the sugar and cinnamon. Take the doughnut sticks out of the air fryer and roll them in the cinnamon-sugar mix. Rep with the rest of the dough.

Notes from the Chef:

Doughnut sticks may also be filled with sugar, butter, melted chocolate, caramel, or some other preferred frosting. Using a box of big refrigerated biscuits (16.3 ounces) to make donut bites. Cut each biscuit into quarters, butter them, and bake them like doughnut sticks. This recipe makes 32 bites.

13.In an air fryer, make a chocolate cake

Preparation time: 10 minutes

Cooking time:15 minute

Servings:4

Ingredients

- Spray for cooking

- a quarter cup of white sugar

- 12 tablespoons of butter

- 1 egg

- 1 tablespoon apricot preserves

- 6 tablespoons flour (all-purpose)

- 1 tablespoon cocoa powder (unsweetened)

- Sodium chloride

Instructions

1. Preheat your air fryer to 160 degrees C / 320°F. Using cooking spray, coat a small fluted tube pan.

2. Cream together the sugar and butter with an electric mixer in a mixing bowl until light and fluffy. Mix in the egg and jam until it is well mixed. Mix thoroughly after sifting in the flour, cocoa powder, and salt. Pour the batter into the pan that has been prepared. With the back of a spoon, level the batter's surface.

3. In the air fryer basket, place the pan. Cook for 15 minutes, or until a toothpick inserted in the cake center comes out clean.

14.Shortbread Cookie Fries in the Air Fryer

Preparation Time: 20 minutes

Cooking time: 10 minutes

Servings: 24

Ingredients

- a total of 14 cups all-purpose flour

- 3 tablespoons sugar (white)

- 12 cup butter

- a third of a cup of strawberry jam

- 1/8 teaspoon dried chipotle pepper, field (Optional)

- a third of a cup of lemon curd

Instructions

1. In a medium mixing dish, add flour and sugar. Break in the butter with a pastry cutter until the evenly coated fine crumbs and sticks together. Create a ball out of the mixture and knead it until smooth.

2. Preheat your air fryer to 350°F (190 degrees C).

3. On a lightly floured surface, roll out the dough to a 1/4-inch thickness. Cut into 3- to 4-inch long "fries" with a 1/2-inch deep slit. Sprinkle with more sugar if needed.

4. In the air fryer basket, arrange the fries in a single layer. Cook for 3 to 4 minutes, or until lightly browned. Allow cooling fully in the basket before transferring to a wire rack. Rep with the rest of the dough.

5. Using the back of a spoon, press strawberry jam through a fine-mesh sieve to make strawberry "ketchup." Stir in the chipotle powder. To make the "mustard," whip the lemon curd until it has a dippable consistency.

6. Sugar cookie fries can be eaten with strawberry ketchup and lemon curd mustard.

15.French Toast Sticks in the Air Fryer

Preparation time:10 minutes

Cooking time:10 minutes

Servings:2

Ingredients

- 4 slices thick, slightly stale bread, similar to Texas toast

- Paper made of parchment

- 2 lightly pounded eggs

- a quarter-cup of milk

- 1 tablespoon Extract of vanilla

- 1 tablespoon of Cinnamon is a spice.

- 1 tablespoon of nutmeg powder

Instructions

1. Cut each slice of bread into quarters to make the sticks.

2. Split parchment paper to suit the rim of the air fryer bas ket.

3. Preheat the air fryer to 180 degrees C / 360°F.

4. In a mixing bowl, whisk together the eggs, cinnamon, milk, vanilla extract, and nutmeg until well mixed. Make sure each piece of bread is fully submerged in the egg mixture. Shake each breadstick to extract any excess

liquid before putting it in the air fryer basket in a single layer. If possible, cook in batches to prevent overcrowding the fryer.

5. Cook for 5 minutes, then switch the bread pieces and cook for another 5 minutes.

16.S'mores of Peanut Butter and Jelly in the Air Fryer

Preparation time: 5 minutes

Cooking time: 5 minutes

Servings: 1

Ingredients:

- 1 peanut butter cup with a chocolate coating

- 2 squares of chocolate graham cracker, divided

- 1 teaspoon raspberry jam (seedless)

- 1 marshmallow, big

Instructions

1. Preheat the air fryer to 200 degrees Celsius (200 degrees C) / 400 degrees Fahrenheit.

2. Place 1 graham cracker square on top of a peanut butter cup. Serve with jelly and marshmallows on top. Place carefully in the air fryer basket.

3. Cook for 1 minute in a preheated air fryer until marshmallows are lightly browned and softened. Top with the remaining graham cracker square right away.

4. Please keep in mind that multiple s'mores can be made at once; just make sure they aren't overcrowded in the air fryer basket.

17.Chocolate Chip Cookie Bites in the Air Fryer

Preparation time 10 minutes

Cooking time:30 minutes

Servings:17

Ingredients:

- 12 cups softened butter

- 12 cups brown sugar, packed

- a quarter cup of white sugar

- 12 teaspoon baking soda

- 12 teaspoon salt

- 1 egg

- 12 teaspoon vanilla extract

- a total of 13 cups all-purpose flour

- 1 cup semisweet chocolate chips, miniature

Instructions

1. To fit an air fryer basket, cut a piece of parchment paper to fit.

2. In a big mixing bowl, beat butter for 30 seconds at medium to high speed with an electric mixer. Mix in brown sugar, white sugar, baking soda, and salt for 2 minutes on medium pressure, scraping bowl periodically. Combine the egg and vanilla extract in a mixing bowl. Blend in as much flour as possible. Combine any leftover flour, chocolate chips, and pecans in a mixing bowl.

3. Put dough 1 inch apart onto parchment paper. Move the parchment paper to the air fryer basket with care.

4. Preheat the air fryer to 300 degrees F (150 degrees C) and cook for around 8 minutes, or until golden brown and set. Cool the parchment paper on a wire shelf. Rep with the rest of the cookie dough.

Notes from the Chef:

It is not recommended to preheat the air fryer for this recipe because the parchment paper will not remain in place.

The dough can also be frozen in portions on parchment paper. Move the dough to a resealable freezer container, mark it, and freeze it for up to a month. When the dough is frozen, add 2 minutes to the cooking time.

18. Apple Cider Donut Bites from the Air Fryer

Preparation Time: 20 minutes

Cooking time: 30 minutes

Servings: 21

Ingredients

- 2 and a half cups all-purpose flour

- 3 tablespoons of granulated sugar

- 4 tablespoons baking powder

- 12 tablespoons apple pie spice

- 12 teaspoon salt

- 1 jar unsweetened applesauce (4 oz.)

- 12 cup apple cider (sparkling)

- 14 cups unsalted butter(melted and cooled)

- 1 huge egg

- 1 teaspoon of apple cider vinegar

Glaze consists of

- 2 cups sugar (powdered)

- 12 teaspoon apple pie seasoning

- 14 cup apple cider (sparkling)

- 1 teaspoon caramel flavoring (optional)

Instructions

1. Preheat the air fryer for 5 minutes at 400 degrees F (200 degrees C).

2. Add flour, apple pie, sugar, baking powder, seasoning, and salt in a large mixing bowl. In a mixing bowl, combine all of the ingredients.

3. Combine melted butter, egg, applesauce, sparkling apple cider, and vinegar in a small mixing bowl. With a spatula, mix the wet and dry ingredients until just mixed. Fill each cavity of the silicon donut mold with 2 tablespoons of batter using a spring-hinged ice cream scoop. In the air fryer basket, put the mold.

4. Reduce the temperature to 350°F (175°C) and cook for 8 minutes. Cook for an additional 2 minutes after carefully turning out the donut bites.

5. When the donut bites are finished, remove them from the basket and cool fully on a wire rack before glazing them, about 30 minutes.

6. Mix icing sugar and apple pie seasoning in a small cup. To make the glaze, whisk together all the caramel extract and apple cider until smooth.

7. Each donut bite should be dipped in a glaze and rolled around to cover both sides.

8. Enable the glaze to dry and harden on a wire rack before serving.

19.Beignets cooked in an air fryer

Preparation time: 10 minutes

Cooking time:15-minute timer

Number of servings: 10

Ingredients

- Spray for cooking

- 12 cup flour (all-purpose)

- a quarter cup of white sugar

- 1/8 cup water

- 1 big separated egg

- 12 teaspoon of butter that has been melted

- 12 teaspoons of powdered sugar

- 12 teaspoon Extract of vanilla

- 1 teaspoon of salt

- 2 tablespoon Sugar for confectioners

Instructions

1. Preheat the air fryer to 370°F (185 degrees C). Using nonstick cooking spray, coat a silicone egg-bite mold.

2. Combine egg yolk, butter, baking powder, flour, sugar, water, vanilla extract, and salt in a large mixing bowl.

3. To combine, mix all.

4. In a small mixing bowl, beat egg whites on medium speed with an electric hand mixer until soft peaks form. Toss into the batter. Using a small hinged ice cream scoop, scoop batter into the prepared mold.

5. Fill the silicone mold and put it in the air fryer basket.

6. Cook for 10 minutes in a preheated air fryer. Carefully remove the mold from the basket; pop the beignets out and turn them over onto a paper round.

7. Return the beignets to the air fryer basket on the parchment round. Cook for another 4 minutes. Dust the beignets with confectioners' sugar after removing them from the air fryer basket.

Chapter-5: Lunch Recipes

1.Pancake Lunch Special

Time to prepare: 15 minutes

Cooking time: 15 minutes

Servings: 4

Ingredients

- 2 cups peeled and deveined tiny shrimp

- 2-quart salsa

- 1 gallon of milk

- 1 pound of flour

- 6 whisked eggs

- 2 tablespoons melted butter

Instructions

1. Preheat the air fryer to about 400 degrees F, put the tray inside, and melt a tablespoon of butter.

2. In a mixing bowl, whisk together the eggs, flour, and milk. Pour into the air fryer's tray, scatter, and cook for about 12 minutes at 350 degrees.

3. Toss the shrimp with the salsa in a cup, mix well, and serve alongside the pancakes. Have fun!

2.Shrimp Croquettes for Lunch

Time to prepare: 15 minutes

Cooking time: 10 minutes

Servings: 6

Ingredients

- 4 tablespoon of extra virgin olive oil

- 1 teaspoon dried basil

- season with salt and black pepper

- 4 chopped green onions

- 2 and 12 tablespoons of lemon juice

- 2 whisked eggs

- 1 pound of bread crumbs

- 1 pound fried, peeled, deveined, and chopped shrimp

Instructions

1. In a mixing bowl, combine half of the bread crumbs, lemon juice, and egg.

2. In a large mixing bowl, combine the basil, green onions, shrimp, salt, and pepper.

3. In a separate cup, combine the remaining bread crumbs with the oil and toss well.

4. Shape circular balls out of the shrimp mixture, dredge them in bread crumbs and cook at 400 degrees F for around 8 minutes in a preheated air fryer.

5. Serve them with a sauce for lunch. Have fun!

3.Fritters with Squash

Preparation time: 15 minutes

Cooking time: 10 minutes

Servings: 5

Ingredients

- 4 tablespoon of extra-virgin olive oil

- 1 cup of baking bread crumbs

- 2/3 cup grated carrot

- 2 grated yellow summer squash

- Season with black pepper and salt

- 1 teaspoon of dried oregano

- 2 whisked eggs

- 5 oz of cream cheese

Instructions

1. In a mixing bowl, combine the pepper, salt, egg, oregano, carrot, breadcrumbs, and squash with the cream cheese.

2. Form tiny patties out of the mixture and coat them in oil.

3. Put the squash patties in your air fryer and cook for approximately 7 minutes at 400 degrees F.

4. Serve them hot for lunch. Have fun!

4.Tortillas with tuna and zucchini

Preparation time: 15 minutes

Cooking time: 15 minutes

Servings: 5

Ingredients

- 2 cups grated cheddar cheese

- 4 tablespoons Mustard

- 2/3-gallon mayonnaise

- 2 cups shredded zucchini

- 8 oz. drained canned tuna

- 6 tablespoons of softened butter

- 6 corn tortillas

Instructions

1. Rub the tortillas with butter, then place them in the bucket of your air fryer and bake for 3 minutes at 400 degrees F.

2. Meanwhile, in a mixing bowl, add the tuna, zucchini, mayonnaise, and mustard.

3. Break this mixture between each tortilla, top with cheese, roll tortillas, place them back in the air fryer basket, and cook for another 4 minutes at about 400 degrees F.

4. Have a meal for lunch. Have fun!

5.Gnocchi for lunch

Preparation time: 15 minutes

Cooking time: 20 minutes

Servings: 5

Ingredients:

- 10 oz. pesto (spinach)

- grated parmesan cheese (half cup)

- 18 oz gnocchi

- 4 minced garlic cloves

- 2 tablespoons extra virgin olive oil

- 2 chopped yellow onions

Instructions

- Heat the olive oil in a fryer pan, then add the onion, gnocchi, and garlic, stirring to combine. Put the pan in the air fryer and cook for about 10 minutes at 400 degrees F.

- Add the pesto, toss well, and cook for another 7 minutes at 350 degrees F.

- Divide into individual dishes and serve for lunch. Have fun!

6.Pizzas for a Quick Lunch

Preparation time:15 minutes

Cooking time: 10 minutes

Servings: 5

Ingredients

- 2 cup sliced grape tomatoes

- 4 cups grated mozzarella

- 4 chopped green onions

- 1 teaspoon dried basil

- 5 oz. sliced jarred mushrooms

- 1 pizza sauce cup

- 2 tablespoons extra virgin olive oil

- 5 pita bread

Instructions

1. Spread some pizza sauce on each pita bread, top with green basil and onions, cut the mushrooms, and top with cheese.

2. Fill the air fryer halfway with pita pizzas and cook for 7 minutes at 400 degrees F.

3. Top each pizza with tomato slices, divide between plates, and serve. Have fun!

7.Stuffed Mushrooms

Preparation time:15 minutes

Cooking time: 25 minutes

Servings: 5

Ingredients

- teaspoon rosemary, finely chopped

- a third of a cup of bread crumbs

- 2 cups broken spinach

- 7 teaspoons grated parmesan

- (half cup) Ricotta cheese

- 2 tablespoons extra virgin olive oil

- 5 Portobello mushroom caps, large

Instructions

1. Brush the mushroom caps with a little oil, position them in the air fryer bowl, and cook for about 2 minutes at 350 degrees F.

2. Meanwhile, in a mixing bowl, combine half of the parmesan cheese with ricotta, spinach, bread crumbs, and rosemary.

3. Fill the mushrooms with this mixture, top with the remaining parmesan, return to the air fryer basket, and cook for about 10 minutes at 350 degrees F.

4. Divide them into plates and serve them for lunch with a side salad of your choosing. Have fun!

8.Veggie Toast

Preparation time:15 minutes

Cooking time: 20 minutes

Servings: 5

Ingredients

- 1 cup crumbled goat cheese

- 4 tablespoons of softened butter

- 5 slices of bread

- 2 tablespoons extra virgin olive oil

- 4 sliced green onions

- 2 chopped yellow squash

- 2 cup sliced crème mushrooms

- 2 red bell peppers, thinly sliced

Instructions

1. Toss the red bell pepper, mushrooms, green onions, squash, and oil in a bowl, then transfer to your air fryer and cook for around 10 minutes at 350 degrees F, shaking the fryer once before transferring to a bowl.

2. Spread the butter on the bread slices, put them in an air fryer, and cook for 5 minutes at 350 degrees F.

3. Break the veggie mix between each bread slice, top with crumbled cheese, and eat for lunch. Have fun!

---

9. Egg Rolls for Lunch

Preparation time:15 minutes

Cooking time: 20 minutes

Servings: 5

Ingredients

- cornstarch, 2 tablespoons
- 2 whisked eggs
- 10 wrappers for egg rolls
- 4 tablespoons Soy sauce
- 4 chopped green onions
- 1 cup grated zucchini
- 1 cup grated carrots
- 1 cup chopped mushrooms

Instructions

1. In a mixing bowl, combine the mushrooms, carrots, green onions, zucchini, and soy sauce.

2. Put egg roll wrappers on a cutting board, cut veggie mix onto each, and roll tightly.

3. Whisk together the cornstarch and egg in a cup, then brush the egg rolls with the mixture.

4. Seal the edges, then place all of the rolls in your preheated air fryer and cook for 15 minutes at 370°F.

5. Assemble them and serve them on a large plate for lunch. Have fun!

10.Air Fryer Party Meatballs

Preparation time: 3-4 minutes

Cook Timing: 15 mins

Servings: 2

Ingredients

- 1 lb. Mince Beef

- ¾ Cup Tomato Ketchup

- 1 tablespoon Lemon Juice

- 1 tablespoon Tabasco

- 2 tablespoon Worcester Sauce

- ¼ Vinegar

- 3 Gingersnaps crushed

- ½ Teaspoons Dry Mustard

- ½ Cup Brown Sugar

Instructions

1. Place the seasonings in a wide mixing bowl and blend properly enough that it is uniformly coated.

2. In the bowl, Add the mince and mix properly.

3. Form into med-sized meatballs and put them in the Air Fryer.

4. Cook for 15 mins on 375F.

5. Before serving, put them on sticks.

11. Air-Fryer Ground Beef Wellington

Preparation time: 3-4 minutes

Cooking time: 20 minutes

Servings: 2

Ingredients

- 1 tablespoon of Butter

- 2 teaspoons of all-purpose flour

- 1/4 teaspoons, Pepper divided.

- 1/2 cup half-&-half cream

- 1 large egg yolk

- 2 tablespoons of finely chopped onion

- 1/4 teaspoons of Salt

- 1/2 lb. Ground beef

- 4 ounces refrigerated crescent rolls

- 1 large egg, lightly beaten optional.

- 1 teaspoon dried parsley flakes

- 1/2 cup Chopped fresh mushrooms

Instructions

1. Preheat the fryer to 300 degrees. Heat the butter over med-high heat in a saucepan. Add mushrooms; cook & mix for 5-6 mins until soft. Stir in the flour and 1/8 teaspoon tablespoon of pepper till combined. Add cream gradually. Put to a boil; cook & stir until thickened, or for 2 mins. Remove & set aside from the heat.

2. Combine egg yolk, 2 tablespoons of mushroom sauce, onion, salt, and 1/8 teaspoon of pepper left in a bowl. Crumble the beef over the mixture and blend properly. Shape into two loaves. Unroll and separate the crescent dough into two rectangles; press the perforations to close. Place each rectangle with the meatloaf. Bring together the edges & pinch to seal. Brush the beaten egg if desired.

3. In the air-fryer basket, put the Wellingtons in one layer on the oiled tray. Cook until a thermometer placed into the meatloaf reads 160 degrees, 18-22 mins, till golden brown.

4. Meanwhile, over less heat, heat the remaining sauce; mix in the parsley. With Wellingtons, serve the sauce.

12. Air-Fryer Sweet and Sour Pork

Preparation time: 5 minutes

Cooking Time: 7-8minutes

Servings: 2

Ingredients

- 1/2 cup, undrained Unsweetened crushed pineapple

- 1/2 cup Cider vinegar

- 1/4 cup Sugar

- 1/4 cup packed dark brown sugar

- 1/4 cup Ketchup

- 1 tablespoon Reduced-sodium soy sauce

- 1-1/2 teaspoon of Dijon mustard

- 1/2 teaspoon of Garlic powder

- (3/4 lb) Pork tenderloin (1 halved)

- 1/8 teaspoons salt

- 1/8 teaspoons of Pepper

- Optional sliced green onions

- Cooking spray

Instructions

1. Combine the 1st 8 ingredients in a saucepan. Get it to a boil; lower the heat. Simmer it uncovered, till thickened, 6 to 8 mins, occasionally stirring.

2. Preheat the fryer to 350 degrees. Sprinkle salt & pepper on the pork. Place the pork in the air-fryer basket on a greased tray; spritz with the cooking spray. Cook for 7-8 mins before the pork starts to brown around the edges. Pour two tablespoons of sauce over the pork. Cook until at least 145 ° is read by a thermometer placed into the pork, 10 to 12 mins longer. Let the pork stand before slicing for 5 mins. Serve with the sauce that remains. Top with the sliced green onions if needed.

Chapter-6: Dinner Recipes

1.Air Fryer Tender Juicy Smoked BBQ Ribs

Preparation time: 10

Cooking time: 20 mins

Servings: 4

Ingredients

- Ribs one rack
- Liquid smoke 1 tablespoon
- Pork rubs 2-3 tablespoon
- Salt & pepper
- 1/2 cup BBQ sauce

Instructions

1 Remove membrane from the back of ribs. It's a tinny layer that is not easy to remove. Occasionally it will be peeled right off. Easily you can cut & peel off. Cut the ribs in the center so that the ribs can easily adjust in the air fryer.

2 Sprinkle liquid smoke on each side of the ribs.

3 Flavor each side with pork rub, pepper & salt.

4 Cover ribs & let ribs at room temp for thirty minutes.

5 Put ribs in an air fryer.

6 Cook for fifteen minutes at 360 degrees.

7 Open-air fryer. Turn the ribs. Cook for an extra fifteen minutes.

8 Remove ribs from air fryer. Sprinkle ribs with the BBQ sauce.

2.Easy Air Fryer Chicken and Cheese Taco Quesadillas

Preparation time: 5 minutes

Cooking Time: 6 minutes

Servings: 4

Ingredients

- Soft tortilla shells 4
- 8-10 ounces of Cooked shredded /cubed chicken.
- 1 teaspoon of Chili powder
- 1 teaspoon of Cumin
- 1 cup of Shredded cheese
- ¼ cup Chopped onion
- ¼ cup Chopped tomatoes

Instructions

1 Flavor the chicken with chili powder & cumin. If not used, cooked rotisserie will have flavor chicken with pepper & salt.

2 Line air fryer with the tortilla shell. Not use any oil in the basket & quesadilla does not stick to the basket.

3 Put ½ cup cheese on the tortilla.

4 The following number put all of the remaining ingredients: first onion, then tomatoes & at the end, chicken.

5 Top with one extra tortilla

6 Cook for three minutes at 370 degrees.

7 Open air fryer & flip quesadilla.

8   Cook for extra three minutes. Must be cook for a long time so that the cheese will melt & if you want crunchy quesadillas, then cook for a long time.

9   Remove quesadilla from the air fryer. Slice it & serve.

3.Perfect Personal Pizzas in an Air Fryer

Preparation time: 5 minutes

Cook Timing: 5 minutes

Servings: 1

Ingredients

- Stonegate Mini Naan

- 2 tablespoons of Jarred pizza sauce

- 2 tablespoons of Shredded pizza cheese

- 6 /7 Mini Pepperoni

Instructions

1   Mini naan will top with pizza sauce in a round, mini pepperoni & shredded pizza cheese.

2   Put the topped pizza in the basket of the air fryer.

3   Adjust air fryer to around 375 degrees F.

4   "Fry" pizza for around five to seven minutes/ till cheese is melted & starts to brown. Serve instantly.

4.Chipotle Steak Tacos

Preparation time: 5minutes

Cook Timing: 8 minutes

Servings: 4

Ingredients

The Steak

- Flank steak 1.5 lbs.

- Red Onion 1/2 cup

- Garlic 2 cloves crushed & peeled.

- Chipotle Chile in Adobo Sauce 1

- 1 tablespoon Ancho Chile Powder

- 1 teaspoon Ground Cumin

- 1 teaspoon Dried Oregano

- 1 tablespoon Olive Oil

- 1.5 teaspoon kosher Salt

- Ground Black Pepper 1/2 teaspoon

- 2 tablespoons of water

For Serving

- 1 cup Salsa

- Tortillas 8 flour, tortillas 6-inch, warmed

- 1/2 cup, Cotija cheese crumbled

Instructions

1 Put beef strips in the large bowl/ resealable bag of plastic. In the blender/ food processor, mix chipotle chile, onion, oregano, chile powder, garlic, cumin, olive oil, water, pepper, adobo sauce & salt. Blend till smooth. Put marinade on meat & mix/ seal bag & massage bag to thoroughly coat & mix. Marinate at room temp for thirty minutes/cover & refrigerate for twenty-four hours.

2 Use tongs, remove beef strips from the bag & lay the basket of an air fryer. Minimize overlap as possible; remove marinade. Adjust air fryer at 400°F for eight minutes, flip beef strips in the center thru cooking time. Do this in the batches.

For the oven

1 Put a steak on the sheet pan in a single layer.

2 Adjust oven to the broil & cook steak for three to four minutes.

3 Turn & allow cook for an extra two minutes.

5.Cilantro Pesto Chicken Legs

Preparation time: 8 minutes

Cooking Time:12 minutes

Servings: 2

Ingredients

- Chicken drumsticks 4

- 1/2 cup Cilantro

- ½ Jalapeño Peppers

- 8 cloves of Garlic

- Ginger 2 thin slices

- 2 tablespoons of Oil

- 2 tablespoons of Lemon Juice

- 1 teaspoon Kosher Salt

Instructions

1. Put drumsticks in the flat tray. Use the sharp knife's tip, cut small slashes in the chicken at steady intervals so the marinade can easily penetrate the chicken.

2. Equally chop pepper, ginger, cilantro, garlic & put them in a bowl.

3. Put oil, salt & lemon juice in the chopped vegetables & combine well.

4. Spread this combination on the chicken.

5. Allow chicken to marinate for at least thirty minutes / up to twenty-four hours in the refrigerator.

6   When completely ready to cook, put chicken legs in the air fryer basket; skin must be side up.

7   Adjust the air fryer at 390F for twenty minutes for the meaty legs of chicken. In the center, turn the legs of the chicken over.

8   Use a meat thermometer to confirm that the chicken has touched the internal temp of 1650F. Remove & serve with sufficient napkins.

6.Crispy Pork Belly

Preparation time: 5 minutes

Cooking Time: 30 minutes

Servings: 4

Ingredients

- 1 lb. Pork belly

- 3 cups Water

- 1 teaspoon of Kosher Salt

- 1 teaspoon of Ground Black Pepper

- 2 tablespoon of Soy Sauce

- 2 Bay Leaves

- 6 cloves Garlic

Instructions

- Cut pork belly into three thick chunks so that it can cook evenly.

- Put all of the ingredients in the inner liner of the air fryer. Cook pork belly at maximum pressure for fifteen minutes. Let the pot sit for ten minutes & release the remaining pressure. Use a set of tongs, cautiously remove meat from the pressure cooker. Let meat drain & dry for ten minutes.

- Cut every three chunks of the pork belly into two long slices.

- Put pork belly slices in the basket of air fryers. Adjust air fryer at 400°F for fifteen minutes/ till fat on pork belly has been crisped & then serve.

7.Air Fryer Scallops | Tomato Basil Scallops

Preparation time: 5 minutes

Cooking Time: 10 mins

Servings: 2

Ingredients

- 3/4 cup Heavy Whipping Cream

- 1 tablespoon Tomato Paste

- 1 tablespoon of Chopped fresh basil

- 1 teaspoon Minced Garlic

- 1/2 teaspoon Kosher Salt

- 1/2 teaspoon Ground Black Pepper

- 12 oz Frozen Spinach

- 8 Jumbo sea scallops

- Cooking Oil Spray

- Extra salt & pepper to season scallops

Instructions

1. Spray seven inches in a heatproof pan & put the spinach in an equal layer at the bottom.

2. Spray each side of scallops with the vegetable oil, drizzle with little salt & pepper on it & place scallops in a pan on the top of spinach.

3. In the bowl, combine tomato paste, garlic, pepper, salt, basil, spinach & scallops.

4. Adjust the air fryer at 350F for ten minutes till scallops are thoroughly cooked through an internal temp of 135F & the sauce is hot & bubbling. Serve instantly.

8.Air Fryer Chicken Jalfrezi

Preparation time: 3 minutes

Cooking Time: 15 minutes

Servings: 4

Ingredients

- Boneless Chicken Thighs 1 lb. & cut it into large, two-inch pieces.

- Onions chopped 1 cup.

- Chopped Bell Peppers 2 cups

- Oil 2 tablespoon

- Kosher Salt 1 teaspoon

- 1 teaspoon of Turmeric 1 teaspoon

- Garam Masala

- Cayenne Pepper 1/2-1 teaspoon

For the Sauce

- 1/4 cup of Tomato sauce

- 1 tablespoon of Water

- 1 teaspoon of Garam Masala

- 1/2 teaspoon of Kosher Salt

- 1/2 teaspoon of Cayenne Pepper

Instructions

1 In the bowl, combine onions, pepper, chicken, salt, oil, garam masala, turmeric & cayenne.

2 Put vegetables & chicken in the basket of an air fryer.

3 Adjust the air fryer at 360F for fifteen minutes. Mix & toss midway through cooking time.

4 In the meantime, make the sauce: In a microwave bowl, mix water, cayenne, garam masala & tomato sauce.

5 Microwave it for one minute. Remove & mix for one minute. Put aside.

6 When chicken is prepared take away & put chicken & vegetables in the bowl. Put prepared sauce on them & toss to cover chicken & vegetables equally with sauce. Enjoy with the naan, side salad/ rice.

9.Tender, juicy smoked BBQ ribs cooked in the air fryer

Preparation time 10 minutes

Cooking time: 30 minutes

Servings: 4

Ingredients

- One rack of ribs
- 1 tablespoon liquid smoke
- 2-3 tablespoon Pork rubs
- a pinch of salt and pepper

- 1/2 cup BBQ sauce

Instructions

1. Peel the membrane away from the back of the ribs. It's a thin coating that's difficult to get rid of. It can be peeled right off on occasion. You can quickly cut and peel it off. Cut the ribs down the middle so they can adjust easily in the air fryer.

2. Brush each side of the ribs with liquid smoke.

3. Season with pork rub, pepper, and salt on each side.

4. Cover ribs and set aside for thirty minutes at room temperature.

5. Put the ribs in the air fryer.

6. Preheat the oven to 360°F and bake for 15 minutes.

7. A fryer that cooks in the open air. Rotate the ribs. Cook for an additional 15 minutes.

8. Take the ribs out of the air fryer. Drizzle the BBQ sauce over the ribs.

10.Chicken and Cheese Taco Quesadillas in the Air Fryer

Preparation time: 2 minutes

Cooking time: 6 minutes

Servings: 4

Ingredients

- tortilla shells (soft)

- 8-10 ounces/cubed cooked shredded chicken

- 1 teaspoon chili powder

- 1 teaspoon cumin

- 1 cup shredded cheese

- 14 cup chopped onion

- 14 cup chopped tomatoes

Instructions

1 Season the chicken with cumin and chili powder. Cooked rotisserie chicken would be flavorful with pepper and salt if not used.

2 Put the tortilla shell in the air fryer. There is no oil in the basket, and the quesadilla does not adhere to it.

3 Spread a quarter-cup of cheese on the tortilla.

4 Add the remaining ingredients, beginning with the onion, then the tomatoes, and finally the chicken.

5 Add one more tortilla on top.

6 Bake for three minutes at 370°F.

7 Remove the quesadilla from the air fryer and turn it. Continue to cook for an additional three minutes. Cook

for a long time so that the cheese melts, and cook for a long time if you want crunchy quesadillas.

8 Take the quesadilla out of the air fryer and set it aside. Serve it cut.

11.Air Fryer Great Personal Pizzas

Preparation time: 3 minutes

Cooking time: 5 minutes

 Serving: 1

Ingredients:

- Round 1 of the Stonegate Mini Naan

- 2 tablespoon pizza sauce from a jar

- 3tablespoon shredded pizza cheese

- 7 Mini Pepperoni

Ingredients:

1 Top mini naan with a round of pizza sauce, mini pepperoni, and shredded pizza cheese.

2 Place the topped pizza in the air fryer basket.

3 Preheat the air fryer to about 375 degrees Fahrenheit. "Fry" the pizza for about five to seven minutes, or until the cheese melts and the crust begins to tan. Serve right away.

12.Tacos with Chipotle Steak

Preparation time:4 minutes

Cooking time: 8 minutes

Servings: 4

Ingredients:

- The Steakhouse

- 1.5-pound flank steak

- 1/2 cup red onion

- garlic cloves, peeled and crushed

- Adobo Chile in Chipotle Sauce 1

- 1 tablespoon of ancho chile powder

- 1 teaspoon cumin powder

- 1 teaspoon dried oregano

- 1 tablespoon olive oil

- 1.5 teaspoon kosher salt

- 1/2 teaspoon black pepper

- 2 tablespoon water

for the sake of serving

- 1 cup salsa

- flour tortillas, 6-inch tortillas, warmed

- 1/2 cup crumbled Cotija cheese

Ingredients

1 Place beef strips in a wide mixing bowl or resealable plastic bag. Combine chipotle chile, onion, oregano, chile powder, garlic, cumin, olive oil, water, pepper, adobo sauce, and salt in a blender or food processor. Blend until fully smooth. Put the marinade on the meat and mix it in, then seal the bag and rub it to coat and mix it thoroughly. Marinate for thirty minutes at room temperature, then cover and refrigerate for twenty-four hours.

2 Remove the beef strips from the bag with tongs and put them in the air fryer basket. Remove the marinade and eliminate the overlap as much as possible. Preheat the air fryer to 400°F for eight minutes, flipping the beef strips halfway through the cooking time. It can be done in batches.

3 To have in the oven

4 Place a single layer of steaks on a sheet pan.

5 Preheat the oven to broil, and cook the steak for three to four minutes.

6 Turn and cook for an additional two minutes.

13.Chicken Legs with Cilantro Pesto

Preparation time: 5 -6 minutes

Cooking time: 20 minutes

Servings:2

Ingredients

- drumsticks of chicken

- 1/2 cup cilantro

- 1/2 jalapeno peppers

- cloves garlic

- thin slices of ginger

- 1 tablespoon of oil

- 2 tablespoon of lemon juice

- 1 teaspoon of kosher salt

Ingredients

- Arrange the drumsticks in a flat tray. Cut tiny slashes in the chicken with the sharp knife's tip at regular intervals so the marinade can easily reach the chicken.

- Chop pepper, ginger, cilantro, and garlic into equal parts and combine in a cup.

- Toss the chopped vegetables with the oil, salt, and lemon juice and toss well.

- Apply this mixture to the chicken.

- Marinate the chicken in the refrigerator for at least thirty minutes and up to twenty-four hours.

- Place chicken legs in the air fryer basket when fully ready to cook; skin side up.

- Preheat the air fryer to 390°F and cook the meaty chicken legs for 20 minutes. Turn the chicken's legs over in the middle.

- Check the internal temperature of the chicken with a meat thermometer to ensure it has reached 1650F. Remove from the oven and serve with plenty of napkins.

14. Pork Belly Crispy

Preparation time: 5 minutes

Cooking time:30 minutes

Servings: 4

Ingredients

- 1 pound pork belly

- 1 cups of water

- 1 teaspoon kosher salt

- 1 teaspoon ground black pepper

- tablespoon soy sauce

- 2 Bay Leaves
- cloves garlic

Ingredients

1 Cut the pork belly into three thick chunks to ensure even cooking.

2 Put all of the ingredients in the Instant Pot/pressure cooker's inner liner. Cook the pork belly for fifteen minutes at high pressure. Allow for ten minutes of resting time before releasing the remaining strain. Carefully remove the meat from the pressure cooker with tongs. Enable ten minutes for the meat to drain and dry.

3 Cut each of the three pork belly chunks into two long slices.

4 Place pork belly slices in the air fryer basket. Adjust the air fryer to 400°F for 15 minutes, or until the fat on the pork belly has crisped, and then serve.

15.Scallops in the Air Fryer | Tomato Basil Scallops

Preparation time:5 minutes

Cooking time: 10 minutes

Servings: 2

Ingredients

- 3/4 cup heavy whipping cream

- 1 tablespoon Tomato Paste

- 1 tablespoon chopped new basil

- 1 teaspoon minced garlic

- 1/2 teaspoon kosher salt

- 1/2 teaspoon black pepper

- 1 12 oz. frozen spinach

- Jumbo sea scallops

- Spray-on cooking oil

- Season scallops with extra salt and pepper.

Instructions

1 Spray a heatproof pan with cooking spray and spread the spinach in an even layer on the rim.

2 Brush each side of the scallops with the vegetable oil, season with a pinch of salt and pepper, and position on top of the spinach in the pan.

3 Combine tomato paste, garlic, pepper, salt, basil, spinach, and scallops in a mixing bowl.

4   Preheat air fryer to 350°F and cook scallops for ten minutes, or until internal temperature reaches 135°F and sauce is hot and bubbling. Serve right away.

16.Jalfrezi (chicken curry) Chicken Jalfrezi in an Air Fryer

Preparetion time:13-14 minutes

Cooking time: 1-2 minutes

Servings: 4

Ingredients

- 1-pound boneless chicken thighs, cut into big two-inch sections
- 1 cup chopped onions
- cups chopped bell pepper
- 3 tablespoons oil
- 1 tablespoon kosher salt
- 1 teaspoon turmeric
- 1 teaspoon Garam Masala
- 1/2-1 teaspoon cayenne pepper

To Make the Sauce

- 1/4 cup tomato sauce

- 1 tablespoon water

- 1 teaspoon Garam Masala

- 1/2 teaspoon kosher salt

- 1/2 teaspoon cayenne pepper

Instructions:

1 Combine onions, pepper, chicken, salt, oil, garam masala, turmeric, and cayenne in a mixing bowl.

2 Put the vegetables and chicken in an air fryer basket.

3 Preheat the air fryer to 360°F and cook for fifteen minutes. Midway through the cooking time, combine and toss.

4 Meanwhile, prepare the sauce: Combine water, cayenne pepper, garam masala, and tomato sauce in a microwave-safe dish. Cook for one minute in the microwave. Remove from the oven and mix for one minute. Delete from the equation.

5 Remove the chicken from the pan and place it in the mixing bowl with the vegetables. Toss them in the prepared sauce to evenly coat the chicken and vegetables. Serve with naan and a side salad or rice.

17.Air fryer Asian-glazed boneless chicken thighs

Preparation time: 5 minutes

Cooking time: 30 minutes

Servings: 4

Ingredients

- 32 ounces, skinless chicken thighs, eight boneless
- 1/4 cup Low sodium soy sauce
- 1/2 tablespoon Balsamic vinegar
- 1 tablespoon Honey
- Garlic three cloves, crushed.
- 1 teaspoon Sriracha hot sauce
- 1 teaspoon fresh grated ginger
- Green one scallion only sliced for garnish.

Instructions

1. In the bowl, mix ginger, soy sauce, honey, balsamic, garlic, honey & sriracha & mix it well.

2. Put half of (1/4 cup) marinade into the bowl with chicken, cover all marinate & meat minimum two hours/ overnight.

3. The remaining sauce will be saved for later.

4   Heat air fryer at 400F.

5   Take chicken from marinade & transfer it to the basket of an air fryer.

6   For fourteen minutes, cook in batch, flip halfway till cooked thru in the middle.

7   In the meantime, put the remaining sauce in a pot & cook over med-low heat till it decreases a little & thickens around one to two minutes.

8   For serving, sprinkle sauce on chicken & top with the scallions.

18. Za'atar lamb chops

Preparation time:5 minutes

Cooking Time:10 minutes

Servings: 4

Ingredients

- 8 Lamb loin chops trimmed

- Garlic three cloves, crushed.

- 1 teaspoon Extra-virgin olive oil

- ½ Fresh lemon

- 1/4 teaspoon Kosher salt

- 1 tablespoon Za'atar

- To taste, fresh ground pepper

Instructions:

1   Lamb chops rub with garlic & oil.

2   Squash lemon on each side & season with zaatar, black pepper & salt.

3   Preheat the air fryer at 400F. Uneven layer & in batches cook to the desired, around four to five minutes on every side.

4   On every bone, chops must have raw meat 2 1/2 oz.

19.Toad in The Hole

Preparation time:20 minutes

Cooking Time: 15 minutes

Servings: 4

Ingredients

- 1/2 cup All-Purpose Flour

- 4 Eggs

- 1 cup Whole Milk

- 1/2 teaspoon Kosher Salt

- 1/2 teaspoon Ground Black Pepper

- 2 tablespoon Dijon mustard

- 2 tablespoons of bacon fat/melted lard(Vegetable oil)

- 4 ounces of Sausages

Instructions

1 In the med bowl, add salt, pepper & flour.

2 Make well in the middle & break in eggs & milk. Beater the eggs & milk & mix gradually into flour. You need batter that is around thick as the batter of a pancake. If it is very dense, put water/ milk. You should cover a batter and allow it to rest until you complete the remaining steps.

3 In a heatproof 6 x 3 pan, put the oil. Sausages should be cut in half & put into oil. Adjust air fryer at 400F for fifteen minutes.

4 Cautiously put in batter on the top of oil & sausages.

5 Adjust air fryer at 360F for twenty minutes/ till batter has been risen & browned on the top.

20.Air Fryer Korean Tacos

Preparation time: 20 minutes

Cooking Time: 10 minutes

Servings: 6

Ingredients

Marinade

- 2 tablespoon Gochujang

- 1 tablespoon Dark Soy Sauce

- 2 teaspoon Minced Ginger

- 2 teaspoon Sugar. /Additional Sweetener Equivalent

- 2 tablespoon Sesame Oil

- 2 tablespoon Sesame Seeds

- 1/2 teaspoon Kosher Salt

- Meat and Vegetables

- 5 lbs. Sirloin beef 1, thinly sliced

- 1 cup, Onion sliced

For Serving

- Tortillas 12 flour, warmed.

- Romaine Lettuce Leaves one head for low carb

- 1/2 cup, cut into 2-inches pieces of Chopped Green Scallions

- 1/2 cup, Kimchi (optional)

- 1/4 cup,Cilantro chopped

Instructions

1   Put sliced onions, sliced beef & green onions into the zip-

top plastic bag. Put soy sauce, gochujang, garlic, ginger, sesame oil, sweetener & sesame seeds. Squish a bag to get meat & sauce to combine well.

2   Let beef marinate at least for thirty minutes/up to twenty-four hours in the refrigerator.

3   Put meat &veggies into a basket of an air fryer. Adjust air fryer at 400°F for twelve minutes, shaking halfway thru.

4   For serving, put little meat in tortillas & top with cilantro, kimchi & green onions.

21.Un-Fried Chicken

Preperation time: 15 minutes

Cooking time: 50 minutes

Servings: 4

Ingredients

- Buttermilk 1 cup

- 1 tablespoon of Louisiana Hot Sauce

- 4, chicken breasts skinless (Boneless)

- Kosher salt/black pepper

- 1/2 cups Breadcrumbs multi-grain panko

- 3 tablespoons grated Parmesan

- 1 tablespoon of lemon zest

- 1 teaspoon Flakes red pepper

Instructions

1 Mix buttermilk & hot sauce in the bowl. Flavor chicken with pepper & salt & dip in a mixture of buttermilk.

2 Mix parmesan, breadcrumbs, red pepper flakes & a pinch of pepper & salt in the dish. Remove chicken from the mixture of buttermilk, allow the extra drip off & dredge in a mixture of breadcrumb until evenly coated. Put pieces flat on the nonstick baking sheet & chill it uncovered at least for 30 mins.

3 Warm the oven to four hundred degrees F. Bake the chicken till just cooked thru, twenty to twenty-five minutes. Split the chicken into four plates & crush the lemon on the chicken.

22.Air fryer hamburger

Preparation time: 5 minutes

Cooking Time: 5 minutes

Servings: 1

Ingredients

- 1 lb. Ground beef
- Ground black pepper.
- Salt

- Cheese four slices

- 4 Burger buns (gluten-free)

- Garnishes

- Tomatoes lettuce

Instructions

1 Air fryer Preheated to 350F.

2 Combine the salt, black pepper & beef in the bowl.

3 Shape the mixture of the beef into four burger patties.

4 Spray the basket of your air fryer t, put in your burgers.

5 Cook for about 8 to 12 mins & flip them mid-way thru cooking.

6 Before 1 min they are completed, take a basket of air fryer & top every burger with the cheese, and turn back to air fryer & cook until completed.

7 Make burgers & now serve them.

8 The doneness of hamburgers by with splendid meat thermometer.

23.Chicken Stuffed with Prosciutto and Fontina

Preparation time:5 minutes

Cooking Time: 10 mins

Servings: 2

Ingredients

- 2 Boneless chicken (breast halves)
- 4 ounces Fontina cheese cut into two inches sticks; rind removed.
- 2 slice Prosciutto
- To taste salt
- To taste ground black pepper.
- 4 tablespoons of unsalted butter
- 2 tablespoons of Olive oil extra-virgin
- 1 cup Portabella sliced mushrooms
- ½ cup Dry white wine
- 3 Rosemary sprigs
- Baby arugula one bunch
- ½, Lemon juiced

Instructions

1 Put halves of chicken breast b/w sheets of the wax paper &, using the rolling pin/mallet, lb. thin.

2 Cover every fontina cheese stick along with the one slice prosciutto & put it in the middle of every half-flattened chicken breast. Roll the chicken around cheese,

prosciutto & secure with the butcher's twine /toothpicks. Flavor chicken rolls along with the salt, black pepper & salt.

3   In the heavy skillet, warm two tablespoons of butter & one tablespoon of olive oil. Speedily rolls of brown chicken on med heat, two to three minutes each side. Put chicken rolls in the air fryer basket. Adjust t temp to 350 degrees & air fry for seven minutes. Remove chicken rolls to the cutting board & allow them to rest for 5 minutes. Cut the rolls at an angle into the six slices.

4   Reheat skillet & put remaining butter, wine, mushrooms & rosemary; sprinkle with pepper & salt; & boil for ten minutes.

5   In a bowl, toss leaves of arugula in the remaining lemon juice, olive oil, pepper & salt. To serve, place chicken & mushrooms on the bed of arugula.

24.Cajun Fried Okra with Creamy Chili Sauce

Preparation time: 20 minutes

Cooking Time: 15mins

Servings: 6 to 8

Ingredients

- Okra

- 1 cup Cornmeal

- 1 cup all-purpose flour

- ½ cup Buttermilk

- 2 lbs. of Fresh okra ½ inch thick sliced

- For spraying, oil

- 1 cup Mayonnaise

- 1 tablespoon garlic chili sauce

- ¼ teaspoon Cajun seasoning

- 1/3 teaspoon ground red pepper

- 2 Teaspoon of Paula Deen's House Seasoning

- Creamy Chili Sauce

- 3 tablespoon Thai sweet chili sauce

Instructions

1   In the med bowl, mix flour, cornmeal, Cajun seasoning & House Seasoning. Put the buttermilk in a bowl. Put okra in the buttermilk, & dredge in the cornmeal combination. Put it on the cookie sheet with the parchment paper. Refrigerate the battered okra for thirty minutes.

2   Working in the batch of ten, spray the okra with oil & place it in the air fryer basket. Adjust temp to four hundred degrees, & air fry for 5 minutes. Mix okra nicely, sprays with the oil, & air fry for five minutes. Mix okra

nicely, sprays with the oil, & air fry for three minutes more. Repeat it with the remaining okra. Enjoy warm with the Creamy Chili Sauce on the side.

3 For creamy chili sauce, add mayonnaise. Garlic chili sauce, Thai sweet chili sauce & red pepper in a bowl & mix well. Cover & chill till ready to serve for 1¼ cup.

25.Air Fryer Fried Rice with Sesame-Sriracha Sauce

Preparation time: 5 minutes

Cooking time: 30 minutes

Servings: 2

Ingredients

- 2 cups cooked white rice

- 1 tablespoon Vegetable oil

- 2 teaspoon of toasted sesame oil

- Kosher salt & ground black pepper

- 1 tablespoon Sriracha

- 1 teaspoon Soy sauce

- 1/2 teaspoon of toasted sesame seeds

- 1 beaten lightly Large egg

- 1 cup & carrots Frozen peas

Instructions

1   Mix the rice, 1 teaspoon of tesame oil, vegetable oil & 1 tablespoon of water in the bowl. Flavor with pepper & salt. Toss to cover the rice. Convert to seven inches round air fryer, insert foil pan & metal cake pan.

2   Place pan in the 5.3-quart air fryer & cook at 350 degrees F, mixing halfway thru, till the rice is slightly toasted & crunchy around twelve minutes.

3   In the meantime, mix soy sauce, sesame seeds, sriracha & 1 teaspoon remaining sesame oil in the bowl.

4   Open-air fryer & put an egg on the rice. Close & cook till egg is cooked thru, around 4 minutes. Again, open it and add carrots & peas; mix in rice to distribute & breakdown the egg. Close & cook for 2 minutes additional to heat carrots & peas.

5   Serve the fried rice into the bowls, sprinkle with a little sauce & sprinkle with extra sesame seeds.

26. Air fryer Falafel Burger Recipe

Preparation time: 5 minutes

Cooking time: 8 minutes

Servings: 2

Ingredients

- Canned Chickpeas 400 g

- Red Onion 1 Small

- Lemon 1 Small

- Gluten-Free Oats 140 g

- Cheese 28 g

- Feta Cheese 28 g

- Greek Yoghurt 3 tablespoon

- Soft Cheese 4 tablespoon

- Garlic Puree 1 tablespoon

- Coriander 1 tablespoon

- Oregano 1 tablespoon

- Parsley 1 tablespoon

- Salt & Pepper

Instructions

1 Put in the food processor/blender all flavors, lemon rind, garlic, drained chickpeas & red onion. Whiz till they are rough but not too smooth.

2 Combine all of them in a bowl with ½ hard cheeses, small cheese, and feta.

3   Mix them all in the form of a burger.

4   Roll all of them in the gluten-free oats till you can't see any chicken mixture.

5   Pu them in the Air fryer, in the fryer's baking pan, cook for eight minutes at 180c/360f.

6   In the bowl, mix the remaining Greek Yogurt, soft cheese, and the additional pepper & salt for burger sauce. Combine all till it becomes fluffy and good. Add the lemon juice & mix one.

7   Put falafel burger inside the homemade buns with garnishes. Add burger sauce to it.

27.Best Ever Air Fryer Vegan Lentil Burgers

Preparation time: 45 minutes

Cooking time: 30 mins

Servings: 4

Ingredients

- 4 Vegan Burger Buns

- 100 g Black Beluga Lentils

- 1 Large Carrot peeled & grated

- 1 Large Onion peeled & diced

- 100 g White Cabbage

- 300 g Oats Gluten Free

- 1 tablespoon Garlic Puree

- 1 tablespoon Cumin

- Handful Fresh Basil & chopped

- Salt & Pepper

Instructions

1. In a blender add gluten-free oats and mix well so that it assembles in each other completely.

2. Put lentils in the saucepan. Cover with the water till they are finely covered. Cook on the med flame for 45 minutes.

3. Same time, put vegetables into Instant Pot & steam for five minutes with steam function.

4. Drain lentils & put them in the bowl with steamed vegetables & oats.

5. Add flavors & shape them into burgers.

6. Put burgers in Air fryer & cook for 30 minutes (180c).

7. Serve with vegan mayonnaise & salad garnish.

28.Air Fryer Persian Joojeh Kababs

Preparation time: 30 minutes

Cooking Time: 15 minutes

Servings: 2

Ingredients:

- 1.5 lbs. Chicken breasts cut into large.

- 1/4 cup, chopped Onion

- 1/4 cup Full-Fat Greek Yogurt

- 1 tablespoon Oil

- 1 teaspoon Kosher Salt

- 1/2 teaspoon Smoked Paprika

- 1/2 teaspoon Ground Black Pepper

- 2 tablespoon Saffron water

- 1 teaspoon Turmeric

Instructions

1 Make a Saffron Water

2 In the mortar & pestle, grind saffron & sugar equally.

3 1/2 teaspoon of this powder is mixed with 1 cup of water to make saffron water so that you can season the cakes, meat, and desserts.

Joojeh Kabobs

1 Put the chicken in the bowl.

2 In a blender, put oil, salt, paprika, Greek yogurt, black pepper, and onion. Blend till you get a smooth mixture.

3 Put all the smooth mixture on the chicken.

4 Add saffron water & turmeric blend till chicken is coated well with the flavoring. Accumulate these two ingredients far ahead to keep the blender bowl from being permanently marked yellow.

5 Let the chicken be left in a marinated bowl for 30 minutes or in the refrigerator until 24 hours.

6 Now remove the chicken from the marinated bowl and put all the chicken in the air fryer basket.

7 Set the air fryer's heat at 370 degrees for 15 minutes, and after that, turn the chicken on both sides to cook well.

8 You must ensure that the meat temperature must be at 165F before it serves.

9 Joojeh kabab will be served with plain rice & butter and saffron water on the rice's top.

Conclusion

One of the 21ˢᵗ centuries outstanding creation is, in fact, air frying; one of the most uprising in popularity, cooking techniques alongside its innovative technology in air fryers

Have become one of the chef's most time saving and smartest tool, it is a brainer this will help take over the worlds cooking industry. In no time, air fryers can assist you in preparing nutritious but tasty meals! To prepare unique dishes for you and acquaintances, you do not need to be a wizard in the kitchen- the air fryer does it all for you!

All you must do is unwind and buy an air fryer alongside this wonderful cookbook on delicious recipes using air fryers!

It is only a matter of time before you tackle the procrastination of tackling the kitchen and make the greatest dishes to dazzle your tastebuds and inspire those around you.

Cooked meals up to restaurant standard, all from the comfort of your kitchen! It is this easy!

Why not opt for a way of bringing outside food within the walls of your home all from the distance of your kitchen while saving energy; it is a win-win. You cannot go wrong! So, pick up an air fryer kit from your local supermarket with this convenient air fryer cookbook to start your journey.